CHER HAMPTON

Healing Your Inner Child First

Becoming the Best Version of Yourself by Letting Go of the Past, Overcoming Trauma, and Feeling Worthy

This book was professionally typeset on Reedsy.
Find out more at reedsy.com

Contents

BONUS: Your Free Gifts

I'm only offering this bonus for FREE to my readers. This is a way of saying thanks for your purchase. In this gift, you will find a guide with extra tools to start your inner journey.

Healing your Inner Child First Guide

Embark on a Transformative Inner Journey to Rediscover Your Inner Child with Extraordinary Tools!

Inside this guide, you'll discover:

1. How to use Journaling in the Healing Process.
2. Questions to Remember Your Inner Child.
3. Space to Write Your Thoughts Down.
4. Questions to Better Understand Your Inner Child's Pain.
5. Motivational Things to Say to Your Inner Child.
6. Positive Affirmations + a 5-Step Method to Make Your Own.
7. An Extra Inner Child Meditation.
8. A Checklist.
9. And More...

To receive this extra **bonus,** go to: https://booksforbetterlife.com/inner-child-first

Or scan the QR code:

Trigger Warning

This book consists of content about trauma, PTSD, and abuse, which may be upsetting to some readers.

Note by the Writer

Many times, I found myself reacting in a certain way that did not fit the situation. I tended to respond highly emotionally on issues that were not that big, leaving me wondering. What happened in that situation? How did we go from 0 to 100 so quickly? Where are these reactions coming from when your responses do not correspond to the situation? Personally, this has been a struggle for me for almost all of my teenage years and earlier adulthood.

My mother and stepfather mostly raised me. My mother was diagnosed with bipolar disorder when I was a little girl. Besides that, my stepfather was mentally and physically abusive to her. When I was seven years old, he committed suicide. As a child, I experienced many stressful life events, making me the person I am today. However, it also made me dysfunctional in some situations that triggered my childhood traumas. When I grew older, I became more aware of my childhood traumas and the resulting triggers of that. I started to gain awareness and dig deeper into the patterns and origin of these behaviors resulting from my traumas.

In my early twenties, I decided to study Psychology with the motivation to help my mother and other people experiencing difficulties in their lives. During my study years, I discovered how important the first seven years of your life are. The fastest development of the human being is between the ages of 0 and 7; the foundation is built between these years, thus extremely important. This made me want to work with this age range to help them to avoid developing dysfunctional behavior in their adult life. However, this will not be useful for adults who are already experiencing difficulties in their lives. This is the motivation for this book, to help people overcome their childhood traumas and problems step by step and start living their best lives.

— CHER HAMPTON

Introduction

"The greater a child's terror, and the earlier it is experienced, the harder it becomes to develop a strong and healthy sense of self"

— NATHANIEL BRANDON

Think back to a time when you were having fun with the other kids in your neighborhood. You tumble and fall while racing around on the playground. The other kids make fun of you. You might not recall everything that happened. You could not even recall who was there or your age at the time. But you remember the embarrassment, the tears in your eyes, and the ache of your skinned knee. You can even recall telling yourself, "I'm never going to make a fool of myself like that again."

Although your knee has healed, you are carrying the wounds into adulthood. You are no longer in command. Your inner five-year-old is still in charge, whether you're twenty or fifty years old. Even though taking a risk may benefit you, you can't forget what occurred on the playground—even if you don't remember it.

When we begin the inner child healing journey, we are tapping into a sensitive and impressionable aspect of ourselves. We may be both the 'grown-up' and the 'child,' offering unconditional self-love, compassion, and support.

We are born with a blank slate. As we mature, we learn everything we will take into adulthood, and we do so in two ways. The first is by gaining experience, and the second is by playing. When we play as children, we act out our experiences, ideas, feelings, and dreams. Our imaginations serve as the foundation for how we prepare for life in the actual world.

Adolescence is a period of exploration, but it can also be a time of suffering. As we get older, we begin to have opinions about the world. Those expectations might let us down at times. We have shattered hearts, we have disappointments, and we have aspirations that never come true. Many of us eventually stop playing and let our experiences define who we are and what we desire.

Heal Your Inner Child in the Following Steps

Self-care is being discussed more often than ever before, and for good reason. Healthcare practitioners and therapists alike are discussing techniques for reducing anxiety and making the current moment as serene as possible. But what do you do when your anxieties, pain, and hurt go much deeper than the present events? How can you begin healing when your inner child is crying out for love, acceptance, and comfort?

Learning to confront the past without allowing it to dictate your present and future might be a difficult step to take, but it is doable. Today, we're going to provide six methods you may use to deal with the problem(s) that caused you to lose your innocence, and begin rebuilding the life you deserve.

1. identify the neglect
2. accept the past
3. accommodate your inner child
4. reach out to your inner child
5. embrace your emotions
6. fill the gap by taking action

How to Develop a Meaningful Relationship with Your Inner Child in Two Steps

ONE: Connect with your inner child, starting a discussion with them, and create a connection.

TWO: Begin to truly listen to and learn about your inner child's needs, sorrows, hopes, and dreams, and take measures to make them a reality.

The objective is for you to tune in to how your inner child is doing, to tenderly care for it, and to discover a method to satisfy its needs. Doing so often clarifies what has to change in order for you to go forward.

Furthermore, this internal process frequently softens the resistance and 'stuckness' you are experiencing in your adult life. Some people find that 'reparenting' their inner child is beneficial in this process as well, using the inner child to alleviate stress and inspire optimism and pleasure.

Let's begin here...

To do this, we will first ask your adult self to be a little more open and potentially vulnerable. Bring your inner kid out of hiding and talk about what's going on or what it requires. We must be open to hearing and witnessing their tale, inquiring about his/her life, hopes, aspirations, anxieties, and problems.

We want your inner child to start building trust with your adult self so that it may share freely. We want to know about its expectations, dreams, wishes, as well as its pain, sadness, fears, and worries.

We frequently notice that when the inner child has someone (adult you) who actually cares, slows down, and is there with them, they can calm down and feel the sensations that he/she has had to suppress for years. It's frequently suggested that you perform this work with a qualified therapist who specializes in inner child therapy, childhood emotional neglect, or emotional difficulties since the work can be delicate. A skilled clinician can guide and support your recovery. However, if you can't see a therapist, don't get disheartened. The approaches outlined in this book will allow you to work on yourself and help your inner child.

As you come to know your inner child better, you may find that they need some serious mending. There are several approaches to providing support, love, and healing to one's inner child. They may need to tell you a narrative that they've been keeping hidden for years. Your inner kid could show you the loss and pain it felt years ago but didn't have the tools to process their trauma. He/she might want to demonstrate to you their need for love and attention, and may want you to discover methods to meet those needs in your life before moving on with the goals you've been concentrating on. They may request that you speak up in your relationships since he/she does not want to be ignored like they were as a youngster. It might also be something else. We have no idea what will come up until we begin this procedure.

When the inner child realizes that you are paying attention to them and trying your best to love it and meet its needs, it will frequently be more accessible to you.

It may need greater physical or emotional safety, more attention to how you're taking care of your mind, body, or soul, recovering from previous wounds, creating boundaries in life, or changing who you spend time with. This effort frequently reveals what is genuinely essential. When we deal with the deeper levels of inner child healing, we've observed how many symptoms are alleviated when clients begin to work beyond and through stuck places. We've witnessed clients begin to open their hearts for the first time, allowing love to enter their lives.

For some, completing the deeper work helps them to be present in their parenting so they can connect without the irritation that was previously there. Others begin to show up to work and relationships with confidence, and they begin to ask for what they require more easily. Others find that their worry and dread have subsided significantly, and they can now stand firm on the limits they've been attempting to establish for years.

Now, our inner kid may either be quiet and comfortable (most of the time), or it can act out and make things a little rumbly on the inside: impeding good relationships, organizational abilities, and self-regulation. When it comes to becoming a contributing member of society, or taking steps toward pleasure, our inner child may make or break us.

If you're feeling irritated or trapped in your life, it's likely that your inner child requires some care. Stuck spots might manifest as difficulty at work, in parenting, in finding or maintaining love, in growing relationships, or in creating boundaries.

> **NOTE**: *This book will have the best effect when you try to perform all the exercises presented in this book to the best of your ability. Sometimes it can also be good to perform them several times; in the end, listen to what feels right for you.*

1

Finding and Reconnecting with Your Inner Child

"A grownup is a child with layers on"

— WOODY HARRELSON

This chapter talks about:

- 9 ways to rediscover your inner child
- Root chakra

As per the definition of the inner child by Woody Harrelson, you may ask if your child within is a real person or only a psychological term or hypothesis. There isn't a physical child inside of you, of course (unless you're pregnant). What you must remember is that, while no one can see tangible indications of your child within, it is still real. We evolve, but our minds and bodies retain memories—and occasionally moods and patterns—from the past. The child within might sometimes be the source of how we feel as adults.

You've undoubtedly mentioned your inner kid a few times before. "I'm channeling my inner child," you could declare while leaping off park swings, chasing your roommate across the house with a Nerf pistol, or plunging into the pool while wearing your clothing.

Many people attribute the idea of an inner child to psychiatrist Carl Jung, who identified a child archetype in his writings (Kellend, 2015). He connected this internal child to memories and experiences of innocence, fun, and creativity, as well as optimism for the future.

Other experts define this inner child as a manifestation of not just your kid self, but also your lived experience through all phases of life (Sjöblom et al., 2016). Because early experiences can have a significant impact on your development as an adult, the inner child can be a source of strength.

Recognizing Trauma

The first step toward healing is identifying the impact of our experiences as children because they continue to have an influence on us in adulthood. Trauma has different effects on each individual, which could include loss of sleep or loss of appetite. One is infused with fear after the trauma and this is one of the ways to recognize it. Childhood trauma, and trauma generally, can manifest itself in a variety of ways. Examples of trauma that may affect kids include (but are not limited to):

- neglect or abuse (whether physical or emotional)
- bullying
- natural calamities
- financial upheaval or hardship

- car mishaps
- substance abuse problems in the family
- other mental or physical health problems in the family
- the loss of a loved one
- domestic violence in the family
- being a displaced person
- housing instability
- predictability is lacking
- distancing from caregivers
- isolation

However, when traumatic childhood events influence you, your inner child may continue to bear these scars until you address the root of the pain.

Recovery

If you were instructed as a youngster not to express your emotions, you may have learned to keep them inside. Though this is only one example, emotional suppression may be harmful both emotionally and physically, thus it is critical to treat it. Lower-level traumas, negative sensations and experiences that have lasting influence are common in childhood. Therefore, even if you are the healthiest child, you can do inner child work to resolve lasting traumas.

Furthermore, if the problem is not identified and addressed while you are still a youngster, major and lasting consequences might occur. The following are some frequent issues in adulthood that individuals address or explore when doing inner child work:

- self-sabotage

- self-destructive conduct
- adolescent passive-aggressive conduct
- anger or outbreaks of rage
- suppression or repression of emotions
- attachment insecurity

With this in mind, it's no surprise that working on your inner child may help you live a better, happier, and more confident adult life. It can help you reclaim your power as a result of childhood adversity and become the person you want to be.

9 Ways to Rediscover Your Inner Child

Relive the simple delight and wonder of existence once more.

Despite that we now know that everyone has a child within. We as individuals occasionally forget to embrace the humorous, lighter side of life. Reconnecting with your inner child involves taking life a little less seriously. Allowing oneself time to play, explore, laugh, and observe the world with delight and astonishment is what this connection implies.

Laughing is a Therapy

Do you recall laughing, even giggling, as a youngster since there was nothing to stop you? You didn't have to worry about expenses or waking up early for work. You lived for the present, and what toy you were going to play with next.

Break out in a huge belly laugh if you wish to release your inner kid. The idea is to laugh as if no one is looking and to be unafraid of doing so. There are many things in life that may make you laugh:

- Consider a humorous situation you've been in. If you've just experienced tragedy in your life, try taking advantage of having a good laugh, it may act as a salve.
- One tried-and-true strategy is to keep pretending to laugh until you start laughing naturally. This is a type of treatment that is used in a variety of institutions, so don't dismiss it. Start laughing right now!
- Spend quality time with your friends, colleagues or family members. Sitting and talking with them can turn any situation into a humorous one. Play games like: I Spy, Slug Bug, and other travel competitions with your family or friends.
- Lastly, you can turn to the internet for a good laugh. Put on a comedy movie or tv show and start laughing your heart out. But remember to not make this an addiction as it may cause negative effects in the future.

Go ahead and be utterly foolish, as the child within connects with your light-hearted and joyful personality. According to the National Library of Medicine, finding opportunities to laugh every day may do wonders for your mental health (Robinson, 2018).

Express Yourself Fully and Honestly

Children appear to express themselves openly via dance, laughter, and play! They also know how to tell it like it is, and may be brutally honest at times!

As you become older, societal standards have a greater influence on your conduct. You may become shy or fearful of expressing yourself. You may speak up less, maybe out of fear of being rejected.

However, your true self deserves to shine! When you don't communicate your actual sentiments, you miss out on important connections and experiences. Learn to talk openly and honestly to re-awaken your inner child. Not everyone will agree with you, and that's fine! When you express yourself, you offer the world your unique perspective, and as a result, attract individuals who actually appreciate you for who you are.

Spend Time with the Kids

Spending more time with children is a great approach to bring out your inner child. Making time to spend with your children, whether you're cracking jokes, running around, or playing games, lets you tap into your inner fun and youthful expression. You will also have the opportunity to share your expertise in order to assist young people in learning and growing. If you don't have children of your own, you might spend time with the children of friends or relatives.

Recognize Your Strengths to Improve Your Inner Peace and Security

Everyone needs to feel safe, especially children. You must build an unbreakable persona that you are confident will protect you. You may do this by being aware of your emotional, physical, and spiritual strengths. Accept that you have obstacles to overcome, and embrace your gift for resilience. If you wish to communicate with your inner child, you must first make them feel protected:

1. Keep an eye out for when you're attempting to modify or deny things that can't be undone. Some individuals interpret warning signs as sentiments such as, "This is unjust, it shouldn't be this

way!" or "Why am I here?" Others may experience warning signals in the form of emotions such as rage or irritation.

2. Remember that "it is what it is," and there is nothing you can do about it right now. Depending on the scenario, you may need to repeat this several times each day/hour/minute.

3. Allow yourself to be sad and dissatisfied; these are useful emotions too! Simultaneously, have faith that acceptance will eventually offer you serenity and tranquility.

4. Seek social assistance. Engage in self-care activities to assist you in coping with tough emotions and improving your mood.

Use Your Imagination

Kids like learning via arts and crafts, dance, drawing, singing, and so on. You, too, may bring out your inner kid via creative activity—and reap several health advantages as a result. Creative self-expression aids in the recovery from trauma, the management of emotions, and the promotion of general well-being (Chen, 2020).

Do you need some motivation? There are several adult coloring books available to help you get your creative juices flowing. Start some do-it-yourself projects to decorate your house or business.

Respect Yourself

Perhaps members of your family adored you and showed it frequently. Even so, a tragic occurrence as a youngster may have made you doubt their love for you. If, on the other hand, your caregivers and other key people in your life rarely showed their affection for you, providing your physical requirements but were emotionally aloof, you may have grown up feeling ignored, unwanted, and maybe even unlovable.

How do you teach yourself to embrace your inner child? As you identify and address your childhood needs, such as emotional needs, social requirements, boundaries, the need to relax, and so on, you will likely begin to notice the benefits of this self-care. It might be difficult at times to recognize what you need and offer yourself the love and respect you deserve. If this describes you, a therapist might be able to assist you in recovering from childhood trauma.

Keep Developing Yourself

Adults are more concerned with problem-solving and completing tasks. Children are eager to study and discover the world's many possibilities. Adults grow more into this fixed mindset where they think they know everything and miss the opportunity to learn. Where children have this growth mindset and always want to discover new things. By letting go of the constant drive to correct and control, you may reconnect with your inner child. Instead, have an open mind and look for learning changes every day.

Consult a Therapist

If reaching out to your inner child causes discomfort or difficult emotions, such as loss, traumatic memories, or feelings of helplessness or dread, be sure to obtain support from a competent mental health practitioner. A therapist can provide support and expose you to coping skills that can help you deal with prior trauma and emotions.

Some therapists may have more inner child work experience and training than others. Inquiring about possible therapists' experience with inner child therapy will assist you in finding the proper individual to support your growth and recovery, as this method is based on the premise that mental health problems, relational issues, and other forms of emotional suffering are frequently the result of unresolved pain or suppressed emotions from childhood and/or adolescence.

In therapy, you may learn to 'reparent' your inner child, which will allow you to start addressing and resolving these difficulties.

Clearing Chakra Blockages

Chakra is a Sanskrit word that means "'wheel' and refers to energy points in your body. They are thought to be spinning disks of energy that should remain 'open' and aligned," as they work in relation to "bundles, major organs, and areas of our energetic body that affect our emotional and physical well-being" (Stelter 2016). These wheels are energy places in your body that become blocked when you experience negativity, pain, or illness.

Root Chakra

Energetically, our "Root Chakra Existence Cycle" of seven years, establishes the basis of who we are throughout our first seven years of life. As a result, our fundamental ideas and unconscious behaviors are formed.

Our energy body develops our root chakra (foundation) as well as all of our other chakras during the first seven years of our life. We have a basic human need that we are attempting to fulfill at each age—one, two, three, and so on. When these demands are addressed, the chakra associated with them tends to open. And if a chakra requirement is not supplied, that chakra tends to close down (Howie, 2021).

Meaning

Our body's most primordial and essential energy center, the root chakra, or Muladhara, is located near the base of our spine, or groin area. The energy here is connected with instinct, survival, and safety and regulated by the root chakra, also associated with the color red.

When the root chakra gets tainted as a result of trauma, psychological difficulties such as persistent dread, or psychosomatic suppression and repression, the flow of life is disrupted. Our clogged energy centers frequently cause us ongoing personal, existential, and relational concerns.

The base layer, 1st Chakra of our Unconscious Mind, serves as a hard drive for the ego. This hard drive stores all of our life streams' cellular memories. These memories are not assigned value when they are recorded, and regardless of whether they are perceived as good or harmful, are saved on the root hard drive of every human person. Whether one was a fetus, an infant, or unconscious when the body was subjected to 'abuse,' the incident was stored in one's memory bank, whether it is recallable consciously or not.

Some people will have terrible memories but will have no idea what caused them or where they originated from. Others will be in shock and will have fully shut off these memories as a coping technique. Others have had great success releasing these memories using emotional clearing techniques such as hypnosis or other therapies. Because our autonomic nerve system and autonomic body processes are controlled by our unconscious mind, unhealed memory trauma in these primary areas causes a wide range of physical symptoms and disease.

Healing

The practice of root chakra healing entails the opening, clearing, purifying, maintaining, and strengthening of the root chakra in our bodies. Root chakra therapy employs certain foods, sounds, scents, affirmations, yoga routines, crystals, and other holistic medicines to restore balance to the body-mind unit.

Obtaining Base Security

To restore balance to our root chakra, we must make a concerted effort to break the fallacy of basing one's self-esteem on the appearance or assumption of external conditions. For many of us, the immediate goal is to be psychologically and emotionally free of being harassed, intimidated, and threatened against one's feeling of inner security, stability, foundation, and well-being. It is entirely up to each of us to maintain that relationship. Only you can create faith in that relationship with yourself; no one else can accomplish it for you.

The root chakra, therefore, is the basis of our body's foundation and our form-holding energetic blueprint, which lives as the holographic tree of life. When we carry unresolved and unconscious suffering in our base frequency, it weakens our whole foundation, eroding the roots that hold our personal tree of life at its very base. Without strong, permanent roots for establishing the strong, secure spiritual basis of one's personal tree of life, one's path may fall or be redirected. This is why laying a solid foundation helps to create a balanced root chakra is crucial in laying a spiritual basis that will help to heal your inner child. When one is not spiritually strong in morals and ethics, one is easily influenced, controlled, or possibly hijacked by controlling forces.

To restore balance to our foundation, we must confront negative archetypes and fear thought-forms in order to deliberately work to change them to a higher frequency of love ideas. At this point, you will be directed to the vibrationally matched and appropriate life route in order to complete the needed learning through the highest awareness pathway.

15 Indicators of an Unbalanced Root Chakra

Pay attention to your ideas, feelings, behaviors, and physical sensations within your body to determine whether you require root chakra therapy.

Here are some red flags to keep a watch out for:

1. You have a tendency to obsess over money. For example, you worry that you don't have enough, you have catastrophic thoughts about going poor and homeless, you overwork to alleviate your financial anxiety, you become triggered whenever someone in your family spends too much, you feel you must have complete control over the money in your family, and so on.
2. You are generally distrustful of people (trust issues).
3. You assume that the only person you can rely on is yourself, and you avoid asking people for favors (even when you really need them).
4. You're a workaholic who burns out easily.
5. You don't get along with your family.
6. You have the impression that there is "never enough" to go around and that you must struggle for what you desire.
7. You're afraid of losing control.
8. You are hyper-aware of any potential threat from people or your

surroundings.

9. For most of the day, you feel dizzy, uneasy, spacey, and ungrounded.

10. You find it challenging and frightening to be your true self in front of people.

11. You are estranged from other people and nature.

12. You're a hoarder who enjoys 'collecting' a large amount of items, resulting in a small and crowded living space.

13. When you are unhappy or stressed, you binge or stop eating totally.

14. You experience issues with your legs and feet, such as: edema, infection, cramping, and poor circulation.

15. The lower part of your body is where you acquire weight the most (e.g. love handles, thick thighs).

How many of the signs on this list do you recognize?

Do You Have an Excessive or Deficient Root Chakra?

When most people talk about 'blocked' or deficient chakras that hinder energy flow, they're talking about diseased root chakras. But do you realize that your chakras may be excessive—or hyperactive—as well?

So, what is the distinction between a deficient and an overactive root chakra? A weak root chakra is considered docile, whilst an overactive root chakra is considered aggressive.

Here's a rundown:
Deficient chakras are: dead, slow, inactive, blocked, and introverted (not enough energy flows in). As a result, you will be more prone to difficulties like worry, distrust, and withdrawal.

Overactive chakras, on the other hand, are: energetic, agitated, reactive, aggressive, and outwardly directed (too much energy flows in). If your root chakra is overactive, you are prone to hoarding, workaholism, greed, and rage.

Hence, excessiveness compensates for deficiencies, whereas deficiency protects. So the question is, which of them do you have? It is also conceivable to fall someplace in between the two categories.

15 Healing Techniques for the Root Chakra

So, how does a healthy and balanced root chakra feel?

When your root chakra is clean, strong, and harmonious, you will feel anchored and tranquil at first. You will no longer be afraid of money or losing control, but will instead come to trust the divine wisdom of life. Not only will you have more faith in yourself, but you will also feel more intimately connected to others and the environment. When your root chakra is in good condition, it will be simpler to be your real self and connect to the calm that is always there in the present moment. You will let go of the need to battle, guard, and defend, and instead align with the ebb and flow of existence.

Root chakra is also great for healing the inner child as the sacral chakra is totally dedicated to this purpose. This chakra deals with creativity and happiness which is essential for your inner child to thrive. In order to reach out to your inner child, practice the following root chakra exercises:

1. **Repeat the phrase "LAM" to yourself:** This sound corresponds to the vibration of the root chakra. You might also want to listen to

binaural beats (a type of music healing therapy that uses alternating sound waves to activate and cleanse all of the chakras). Listening to binaural beats between 7-30 Hz daily will bring a change and help the inner child to heal.

2. **Go for a walk in the woods on a regular basis:** Take conscious notice of your feet's relationship to the soil.

3. **Practice targeted yoga:** Stretch your muscles with the basic yoga poses of child pose, forward bend, mountain pose, squat, and warrior.

4. **Consume grounding foods:** Consider root vegetables such as sweet potatoes, beets, radishes, and others.

5. **Practice mindfulness for 30 seconds:** Make it a habit to pause every day and count your breaths for three counts. This simple exercise will assist you in regaining your footing.

6. **Carry crystals with you and meditate with them:** Use crystals from the root chakra, such as: jasper, hematite, smokey quartz, and carnelian. Black tourmaline is my favorite root chakra gem.

7. **Use aromatherapy smells to cleanse the root chakra:** Sandalwood, vetiver, patchouli, cloves, black pepper, and ginger are some essential oils to try.

8. **Experiment with 'earthing:'** Earthing is the technique of walking on grass or ground to recharge the human energy field.

9. **Sit quietly and envision:** Imagine a crimson ball of light pulsing in your root chakra (your groin area). Consider all of the murky energy dissolving as it comes into contact with the ball of red light.

10. **Set aside time each day to sit outside and connect with nature:** Simply watch what is happening around you: the birds, the breeze, the clouds, the light, and feel your oneness with nature.

11. **Make use of affirmations or mantras:** To change your unconscious thought habits, use mantras or affirmations: "I am grounded," "I am centered and whole," "I trust in the wisdom of

life," "I have all I need," "I am safe and secure," "I surrender," and "I am strong, stable, and at peace" are some affirmation/mantra examples.

12. **Drink a grounding tea:** Include root chakra cleansing herbs such as ashwagandha and cloves.

13. **Take a relaxing shower:** Water has the ability to clear sluggish and obstructed energy. Alternatively, take a cleansing bath with mineral salts like Himalayan pink rock salt.

14. **Look into the source of your anxieties:** Fears arise as a result of your inner beliefs, grudges, and unresolved sorrow. Spend some time in a notebook or with a trusted friend, partner, or therapist, reflecting on the source of your anxieties.

15. **Engage in catharsis:** Every day, engage in catharsis to actively release blocked root chakra energy. You may try dynamic meditation or just leap, kick, punch, yell, or dance your stress away.

Story of Someone Who Has Been Through the Journey

Let's consider for a moment, the story of someone who has previously suffered with a very unbalanced root chakra (Thoughtless Delineation, 2018):

I discovered that incorporating greater awareness into my days helped quickly and tremendously. Slowing down, taking more pauses, and connecting with my breath were all basic and straight-forward initial steps I took. Following that, I began using the other therapeutic methods, such as: aroma therapy, connecting with nature, and journaling for insight and cathartic release.

Childhood trauma may leave an indelible imprint on our minds. These memories might be kept in our bodies, cells, in our very essence. The route to completeness within myself was therefore about providing a safe space for this trauma to be heard and healed.

For those, like myself, who have undergone bodily trauma, the energy toll is enormous. It means that the body is never a safe place to be, and the planet is never a secure place to be. It implies that we do not believe we can fall and be caught. It implies submission may evade us, yet the beauty of surrender is that when we do, we get the greatest blessings in life: love, freedom, joy.

Trauma in the body also means that we are always firing on all cylinders, which can lead to a depletion of resources and energy levels that affect our health on several levels.

I've been fortunate to experience numerous methods of self-knowledge and healing over the years that I've spent learning to own my body and know myself. And this is now influencing the work I share.

My idea is that when we can't figure out why something is the way it is, or why we're stuck in some manner, we turn to the body for solutions. And our body will tell us what is going on.

Many individuals might be in their 30s, 40s, or older, and live very successful lives, but at some level, the terrified kid within them remains frightened. On some level, their bodies are still holding the trauma, and it will have an impact, whether subtle or overt.

Trauma may become such a familiar companion in our body that we may seek out more unpleasant occurrences because the reverse seems incorrect in some way. As a result, many people who come from violent backgrounds may find themselves in similar situations again.

We persist in the pain because we are creatures of habit—familiar equals safe. As a result, the wire tripping persists. However, true comfort comes from teaching the body what is good and healthy.

Key Takeaways

- Don't be afraid of bringing your inner child out as he/she is the one affected. Addressing your inner child will help you to heal.
- Root chakra is the process of healing internally and will help you overcome the trauma. You don't necessarily need to have experienced a traumatic childhood to benefit from this healing— any minor issue throughout life can also be the reason. No matter what it is, the earlier it is addressed, the better it will be for you.
- The fifteen above mentioned techniques are the guide to healing. If you feel like this is new for you, and you feel overwhelmed, keep reading ahead to trust the process.

2

Emotional and Psychological Trauma

"The greatest happiness of life is the conviction that we are loved;
loved for ourselves, or rather, loved in spite of ourselves"

— VICTOR HUGO

This chapter talks about:

• Effects of trauma in childhood and the risk of future trauma
• Aftermath of emotional and psychological distress

Children whose families and homes do not consistently give regular safety, comfort, and protection may develop coping mechanisms that allow them to live and function on a daily basis. For example, they may be highly sensitive to other people's moods, always monitoring to see what the adults around them are feeling and how they will behave. They may hide their feelings from others, never allowing them to see when they are fearful, sad, or furious. When physical and/or mental threats are constant, these types of learned adaptations make sense. As a child grows older and experiences safe environments and relationships, these adaptations become less useful, and may even be counterproductive, interfering with the ability to live, love, and be free.

What occurs to us in our first ten years of life has an impact on every decade that follows. Our bodies, brains, and personalities are imprinted by our early experiences during this very fast era of growth and development. That is why childhood trauma may have such a profound effect on our mental and physical health and well-being throughout our lives. The definition of childhood trauma varies greatly. Childhood trauma can manifest itself in a variety of ways, including physical or sexual abuse, neglect, unstable or hazardous environment, witnessing violence in the household, and serious illness. Furthermore, children might suffer from relational trauma, which is defined as a break in the primary link with a parent or caregiver. Trauma can also be triggered by events outside the home, ranging from intense bullying to the communal trauma caused by catastrophic events such as a pandemic. What influence can childhood trauma have on an individual's capacity to flourish as they grow older? Here are six ways trauma can appear mentally and physically as children move through adolescence into adulthood.

Trauma and Self-Worth

How we are treated by people closest to us from infancy onwards is critical in forming our perception of ourselves as worthwhile and deserving of love and care. Children who are mistreated or neglected by their primary caregivers learn that they are unlovable. Even loving parents who do not relate with their children may accidentally send this message to them. Furthermore, 'parentification' occurs when parents rely on their children to satisfy their emotional needs, and children learn that their own needs are unimportant. As a result, traumatized youngsters acquire a deep feeling that they are unworthy. They may blame themselves for their treatment, feeling that if they were 'better,' their parents would "love them more." Even if this self-perception is unconscious or semi-conscious, it can be exceedingly difficult to change later in life. An individual may finally realize why their parent(s) acted the way they did, maybe as a result of their own unresolved childhood trauma or a mental or physical disease. However, awareness alone may not be sufficient to transform the adult child's self-image and feeling of self-worth.

In turn, this fundamental wound, as it is sometimes called, causes a deep well of emotional suffering. As a result, young people who have experienced childhood trauma and the guilt and shame that comes with it are more likely to suffer from anxiety, depression, and maladaptive coping methods such as substance abuse and self-harm.

Relationships and Attachment

It is impossible to emphasize the value of a child's tight bond with a caregiver. Children learn to trust people, manage their emotions, and engage with the environment through interactions with significant attachment figures; they acquire a sense of the world as safe or hazardous, and they start to appreciate their own value as individuals. Children learn that they can't rely on others to aid them when those close interactions are unstable or unpredictable. When a child's primary caregivers exploit and abuse him or her, the youngster internalizes self-hate and comes to believe that the world is a dreadful place.

The majority of abused or neglected children struggle to form a strong, healthy relationship to a caregiver. It has been demonstrated that children who do not develop healthy bonds are more sensitive to stress. They have difficulty managing and expressing their emotions, and they may respond aggressively or improperly in certain situations. Our capacity to have healthy, supportive connections with friends and significant others is dependent on our ability to form such ties in our families. A youngster who has experienced complex trauma may struggle in romantic relationships, friendships, and with authority figures such as teachers or police officers.

Physical Well-Being: Body and Mind

The biology of the body evolves from birth until adolescence. The environment influences normal biological function in certain ways. For instance, when a kid grows up fearful or under persistent or acute stress, the immune system and stress response mechanisms in the body may not develop appropriately. When the kid is later subjected to even moderate amounts of stress in adulthood, these systems may behave as though the individual is under acute stress. When confronted with stressful events, an individual may exhibit strong physiological reactions, such as: fast breathing, heart pounding, or may "shut down" completely. While these reactions are standard biological reactions to stress, they are often out of proportion in the context of typical stress and appear to the outside world as: 'overreacting,' 'unresponsiveness,' or 'disconnection.'

The development of the brain and nervous system can be hampered by stress in the environment. In neglectful situations, a lack of mental stimulation may prevent the brain from growing to its full capacity. Children who have experienced complicated trauma may have persistent or recurring medical issues, such as headaches or stomach aches. Adults with a history of childhood trauma have been found to have more chronic bodily diseases and issues. They may engage in dangerous activities, exacerbating the severity of these illnesses.

Body dysregulation is a common symptom of complexly traumatized adolescents, meaning they either overreact or underreact to sensory inputs. Some may be hypersensitive to noises, scents, touch, or light, for example, or they may be numb in a manner of speaking, to pain, touch, or internal bodily sensations. As a result, individuals may harm themselves without experiencing pain, suffer from physical difficulties without realizing it, or complain of persistent discomfort in numerous body parts for which no physical explanation can be located.

Emotional Reactions

Children who have undergone severe trauma, frequently struggle to: understand, express, and manage their emotions, and may have limited terminology for experiencing such states. They frequently internalize and/or externalize stress reactions, which can lead to considerable melancholy, anxiety, or aggression. Their emotional reactions might be erratic or explosive. Trembling, rage, grief, or avoidance may be displayed by a youngster in response to a reminder of a traumatic experience. Reminders of multiple traumatic incidents may therefore lurk anywhere in everyday surroundings for a youngster with a complicated trauma history. When disturbed, such a youngster may often respond violently, and have difficulties calming down. Because interpersonal traumas are so common, even minimally unpleasant contact with others can function as trauma memories and cause significant emotional reactions.

Children are typically alert and guarded in their dealings with others, and are more prone to view circumstances as stressful or hazardous, having learnt that the world is a terrible place where even loved ones cannot be trusted to protect them. While this defensive stance is beneficial when an individual is being attacked, it becomes troublesome in situations that do not necessitate such ferocious reactions. Many youngsters, on the other hand, learn to "tune out" (emotional numbness) to hazards in their surroundings, leaving them exposed to revictimization.

Difficulty controlling emotions is widespread and occurs even in the absence of partnerships. Many of these youngsters get quickly overwhelmed because they have never learned how to calm themselves down when they are unhappy. In school, for example, they may feel so upset that they abandon even the smallest activities that provide a challenge. Children who have undergone early and strong traumatic incidents are more likely to feel scared all of the time and in a variety of scenarios. They are also more prone to suffer from depression.

Dissociative Symptoms

Dissociation is common in children who have experienced complex trauma. When children are confronted with an overpowering and frightening situation, they may dissociate, or psychologically remove themselves from it. They may feel disconnected from their bodies, floating on the ceiling or elsewhere in the room, witnessing what is occurring to their bodies. They may believe they are in a dream or another altered condition that is not quite real, or that the event is occurring to someone else. Alternatively, individuals may lose all recollections or sense of what occurred to them, resulting in temporal gaps or holes in their personal history. At its most severe, a youngster may cut off or lose contact with numerous parts of his or her life.

Although children do not naturally disassociate intentionally, once they have learned to as a protection strategy, they may dissociate spontaneously in subsequent stressful situations or when confronted with traumatic memories. As a result, dissociation can impair a child's capacity to be completely present in daily activities and drastically disrupt a child's sense of time and continuity, thus having the potential to impair learning, classroom conduct, and social relationships. Others may not always notice when a child is dissociating, and it may appear that the youngster is merely 'pinging,' daydreaming, or not paying attention.

Effects on Cognitive Abilities

When brain function is interrupted, the consequences are far-reaching. Along with the mental and physical health repercussions of childhood trauma outlined above, individuals might also develop cognitive issues— difficulties with memory, logical reasoning, and problem solving. These executive functioning deficits might make it difficult for individuals to establish goals, plan for the future, and achieve success in academic or professional settings. According to research, those who have undergone childhood trauma have a smaller prefrontal cortex, the area of the brain responsible for executive functioning.

Cognitive deficits can be caused by habitual psychological patterns that a child develops as a result of trauma, in addition to brain structure and function. When youngsters are continually exposed to stress, all of their energies are devoted to surviving the stressor. As a result, they have less energy, attention, and interest to devote to learning, developing new abilities, and making sound judgments. Even after the traumatic experience has passed, trauma triggers, and the ongoing struggle to avoid them, divert a child's efforts and attention away from learning

25

new things. As a result, childhood trauma symptoms and PTSD are linked to the following problems in early adulthood and beyond:

- learning disabilities
- memory problems
- language difficulties
- difficulty with organization and planning
- adults are more sensitive to traumatic stress
- a short attention span
- cognitive abilities deteriorate at a faster rate.

Emotional and psychological trauma is produced by very stressful conditions that rob you of your sense of security, leaving you helpless in a dangerous setting. Psychological trauma can leave you with unresolved unpleasant feelings, memories, and anxiety. It can also make you feel numb, distant, and hard to trust others.

Traumatic situations frequently include a threat to one's life or safety, but any circumstance that leaves you feeling overwhelmed and lonely can result in trauma, even if no physical damage is involved. The subjective emotional experience of the event, rather than the objective conditions, determines whether an incident is traumatic. The more terrified and helpless you feel, the more probable it is that you have been traumatized. Below is a list of some traumatic citations that can cause physical and psychological turmoil:

- major and minor incidents, such as an accident, injury, violent attack, losing a loved one, divorce or bullying, can contribute to emotional and psychological stress
- constant and unrelenting stressors, such as living in a high-crime area, suffering a life-threatening illness, or witnessing horrific

events on a regular basis, such as, bullying, spousal abuse, or childhood mistreatment

- commonly ignored reasons, such as surgery (particularly in the first three years of life), the unexpected loss of a close relative, the end of an important relationship, or a humiliating or severely disappointing event, especially if someone was intentionally harsh

It might be tough to cope with the trauma of a natural or man-made tragedy, even if you were not personally engaged in the event. In reality, while it's exceedingly improbable that any of us would ever be direct victims of a terrorist attack, aircraft accident, or mass shooting, for example, we're all frequently exposed to awful pictures of those who have been on social media and news outlets. Repeatedly viewing these sights might overload your neural system and cause severe stress. Whatever the origin of your trauma, and whether it occurred years ago or recently, you're encouraged to make therapeutic adjustments and go on with your life.

Trauma in Childhood and the Risk of Future Trauma

While traumatic events may happen to anybody, you're more likely to be traumatized by an incident if you're already under a lot of stress, have recently suffered a string of losses, or have previously been traumatized—especially if the previous trauma occurred when you were a child.

Trauma in childhood can have serious and long-lasting consequences. When childhood trauma is unresolved, the child grows up with a sense of fear and powerlessness, setting the framework for future trauma. Even if your trauma occurred many years ago, there are steps you can take to overcome your pain, regain your emotional balance, and relearn to trust and connect with others.

The effects of a traumatic incident usually last a few days to a few months, gradually dissipating as you absorb the upsetting incident. Even if you're feeling better, you may be bothered by unpleasant recollections or feelings from time to time, especially in reaction to triggers like an anniversary of the occurrence or something that reminds you of the trauma.

Whether a traumatic incident results in death, or not, you must cope with the loss. Grief is the normal reaction to this loss. You, like those who have lost a loved one, must go through a mourning process. The following suggestions can assist you in coping with your sorrow, healing from the trauma, and moving on with your life.

Tip 1: Get going!

Childhood trauma alters your body's natural homeostasis, causing you to become hyper aroused and fearful. These sensations stay embedded within your brain causing it to function in a negative way. Staying idle can worsen the situation especially when you are alone and have nothing to do. Exercise and movement, in addition to burning off adrenaline and creating endorphins, can also assist in restoring your neurological system.

- **On most days, try to exercise for 30 minutes or more.** If it's more convenient, three 10-minute bursts of exercise every day are just as effective. Walking, yoga, jogging, swimming, basketball, or even dancing are examples of rhythmic exercises that utilize both your arms and legs.
- **Include a mindfulness component.** Rather than focusing on

your thoughts or distracting yourself while exercising, concentrate on your body and how it feels as you move. Consider the sensation of your feet striking the ground, the rhythm of your breathing, or the sense of wind on your skin. Rock climbing, weight training, boxing, or martial arts can help with this. Remember to focus on your body motions to avoid harm during these sports.

Tip 2: Avoid Isolating Yourself

Isolating oneself after a terrible occurrence may seem like a comfort, but it will only make issues worse. Maintaining relationships and limiting your time alone will help you heal.

- **You are not compelled to talk about the trauma.** Connecting with people does not have to include discussing the trauma. In fact, for some people, this might make matters worse. Feeling involved and welcomed by others provides comfort.
- **Solicit assistance.** While discussing the trauma is not a necessity, it is vital that you have someone with whom you can relate your experiences face-to-face, someone who will listen carefully without judging you. Seek the advice of a trustworthy family member, friend, counselor, or pastor.
- **Even if you don't feel like it, engage in social activities.** Participate in 'normal' activities with other people that have nothing to do with the traumatic incident.
- **Participate in a support group for trauma victims.** Connecting with others who are coping with similar challenges can help you feel less alone, and hearing how others deal with their issues may inspire you to work on your own recovery.
- **Volunteer.** Volunteering, in addition to helping others, may be an excellent method to combat the sense of powerlessness that

frequently accompanies trauma. Helping others might help to remind you of your abilities and restore your sense of power.

Tip 3: Train Your Nervous System to Self-Regulate

It is critical to understand that you can change your arousal system and relax yourself regardless of how anxious, scared, or out of control you feel. It will not only help to alleviate the anxiety associated with trauma, but it will also provide you with a sense of control.

- **Breathing with awareness.** If you're feeling bewildered, confused, or agitated, practicing mindful breathing might help you settle down quickly. Simply take 60 deep breaths, focusing on each 'out' breath.
- **Toning of the voice.** As weird as it may sound, voice tone is an excellent approach to increase social interaction. Sit up straight and make a simple "'mmmm" sound. Adjust the pitch and loudness until you feel a nice vibration in your face.
- **Sensory information.** Is there a certain sight, scent, or flavor that instantly makes you feel calm? Perhaps caressing an animal or listening to music might rapidly calm you down or putting some essential oils on your body? Everyone reacts differently to sensory input, so try out several rapid stress reduction tactics to see what works best for you.
- **Keeping a firm footing.** Sit on a chair to feel more present and grounded. Feel the earth beneath your feet and your back against the chair. Look around you and select six things that include the colors red or blue. Take note of how your breathing becomes deeper and more relaxed.
- **Allow yourself to feel what you need to feel when you need to experience it.** Recognize and embrace your feelings regarding the

trauma as they emerge.

Tip 4: Look After Your Health

It's true, having a healthy physique can improve your ability to cope with trauma-related stress.

- **Get lots of rest.** Worry or fear may disrupt your sleep habits after a distressing encounter. A lack of quality sleep, on the other hand, might increase your trauma symptoms and make it more difficult to maintain your emotional equilibrium. Aim for 7 to 9 hours of sleep every night and go to bed and wake up at the same time every day.
- **Stay away from alcohol and drugs.** Their usage can exacerbate your trauma symptoms and heighten feelings of melancholy, anxiety, and isolation.
- **Reduce your tension.** Try relaxing techniques such as meditation, yoga, or deep breathing exercises. Make time for activities that make you happy, such as your favorite pastimes.
- **Consume a well-balanced diet.** Eating modest, well-balanced meals throughout the day will help you maintain your energy and reduce mood fluctuations. To improve your mood, avoid sugary and fried meals and consume enough of omega-3 fats, such as salmon, walnuts, soybeans, and flaxseeds.

A well-balanced diet provides your body with the nutrition it requires to function properly. To receive enough nourishment, the majority of your daily calories should come from:

- fruits
- vegetables

- lean proteins
- legumes
- whole grains

When Should You Seek Professional Trauma Therapy?

It takes time to recover from trauma, and everyone heals at their own speed. However, if you feel that it interferes with your daily life, you may want professional assistance from a trauma specialist. Seek trauma treatment if you are experiencing any of the following circumstances:

- having trouble working at home or at work
- suffering from intense dread, anxiety, or depression
- unable to build strong, rewarding relationships
- experiencing terrible memories, nightmares, or flashbacks
- stay away from anything that reminds you of the trauma
- emotionally numb and alienated from others
- relying on drink or drugs to cope

Working through trauma may be frightening, difficult, and possibly re-traumatizing; thus, this healing process is best done with the assistance of an experienced trauma specialist. It may take some time to find the proper therapist. It is critical that the therapist you select has expertise in treating trauma. However, the quality of your relationship with your therapist is just as crucial. Choose a trauma specialist with whom you feel at ease. Find another therapist if you do not feel comfortable, respected, or understood. But keep in mind, at the end of the day, therapists are people as well, trying to help you.

Ask yourself the following questions:

- Did I feel at ease expressing my difficulties with the therapist?
- Did I feel as if the therapist understood what I was saying?
- Were my concerns treated seriously, or were they dismissed?
- Was I handled with kindness and respect?
- Do I think I could come to trust the therapist?

Post Traumatic Stress Disorder

If your symptoms do not improve or worsen, and you are unable to move on from the experience for an extended length of time, you may be suffering from Post Traumatic Stress Disorder (PTSD). While emotional trauma is a normal reaction to a terrible event, it progresses to PTSD when your nervous system becomes 'stuck' and you remain in psychological shock, unable to make sense of what happened or process your feelings.

To recover from psychological and emotional trauma, you must: confront unpleasant sensations and memories, release pent-up "fight-or-flight" energy, learn to manage powerful emotions, and regain your capacity to trust others. In a child's treatment for PTSD, a trauma expert may employ a range of different therapy techniques:

Somatic experience is concerned with physiological sensations rather than ideas and recollections of the traumatic incident. You can release pent-up trauma-related energy through shaking, weeping, and other types of physical release by focusing on what's going on in your body.

Cognitive-behavioral therapy assists you in processing and evaluating your ideas and feelings in the aftermath of a tragedy.

EMDR (Eye Movement Desensitization and Reprocessing) combines cognitive-behavioral therapy aspects with eye movements or other types of rhythmic, left-right stimulation to 'unfreeze' traumatic memories.

Things You Can Do That Help in the Aftermath of Emotional and Psychological Distress?

Regression is a typical reaction to trauma, and there are strategies to assist your inner child to move forward and leave it behind. Firstly, you need to think back to a time when you felt safe before the trauma. Younger children may wet the bed or need a bottle, while older children may be afraid of being alone. If your inner child behaves in this manner, it is critical that you be understanding, patient, and reassuring.

Your inner child believes it is their fault. If you experience major or minor traumas at a young age, you don't know how to recover from it and the inner child takes on the blame. Assure your inner child that he or she is aware that they did not cause the incident.

Some individuals have trouble going to sleep, while others wake up frequently or have disturbing dreams. This is all because your inner child feels alone and all these years of bottling up the feelings keeps him/her on edge. Toss a cuddly animal and a warm blanket into your bed to make yourself comfortable. Make sure to have no screen time at least one hour before you go to bed. Try to do something that you find relaxing, like reading or having a bath.

In the following chapters, we will further discuss how you can break free from negative childhood patterns, different phases in the healing process, and how you can let go of the past.

Key Takeaways

- After experiencing trauma, you may keep thinking about it and asking yourself questions like "why me?" or "what could I have done to get out?" So, just remember that the first step to moving on is accepting that it happened and focusing instead on healing.

- Don't forget to take good care of your health amidst inner child healing. Your food intake is directly linked to this healing so make sure you are eating a balanced diet.

- Your inner child is the one who is wounded, so remember to heal him/her to ultimately heal yourself.

3

Breaking Free from Negative Childhood Patterns and Reparenting Yourself

"Seeing unhealthy patterns in your family and deciding that those patterns end with you and not be passed down to future generations, is an extremely brave & powerful decision"

— TINY TAT

This chapter talks about:

- Reparenting your inner child to break the cycle of trauma
- What is shadow work? How this practice can help you live a better life

Reparent Your Inner Child to Break the Cycle of Trauma

The following testimonial demonstrates just how deeply entrenched childhood trauma can become in adult life (Pandey, 2021):

Finally, the extent of my abhorrent behavior had caught up to me. Seeing my son cowering in the corner with unadulterated fear, fear of being yelled at and beaten, felt like a punch in the gut. My anger issues, and my proclivity to violence and infidelity, resulted in failed relationships. My disintegrating marriage, the fear of losing custody of my only child, a child I loved with all my, had finally sunk in. I realized I could not go on like this. I realized I wasn't happy anymore, no matter how hard I tried. It was like I was stuck in an endless loop where similar situations repeated in all the walks of my life. I decided enough was enough. I was going to change this. I was going to dig deeper and give my life a one-eighty degree turn.

The answers to this man's questions lay in his childhood, the family environment he grew up in, the interactions with his parents and peers created the man he had become. Humans are contradictory beings, with both a sophisticated and a basic experience of consciousness. We are a mash-up of every age we've ever been at the same time. We carry the wisdom of our current selves as well as the innocence of our inner kid. People who endured childhood trauma or neglect have scars that have been buried deep inside their subconscious thoughts.

Even persons who grew up in a mostly good atmosphere have the impressions of the terrible experiences they've endured lodged in their mind. Our subconscious mind is created during our youth, particularly between birth to four years of age. It is the time at which we first feel emotions. It is the age when we begin to analyze our emotions, observe our parents' and elders' interactions, learn to set and maintain boundaries, our behavioral patterns, and other nitty-gritty (Pandey, 2021).

Our inner child is a part of ourselves that has been there since we were conceived, through utero and all of the developmental years following when we were young and developing into delicate selves: baby, infant, toddler, young kid, and middle school aged. We all have an inner kid. Your "inner child" is a subconscious part of you that has been gathering up messages long before you were ready to completely grasp what was going on (mentally and emotionally). It contains previous emotions, memories, and beliefs, as well as future aspirations and desires. If you are new to the idea of reparenting your inner child, you may be pondering the following questions:

So, how does this inner child play a role in how we perceive life?

Every person is plagued with troubles in their lives. Some lack the communication skills required for a successful and healthy relationship, others are struggling with harmful habits such as addiction and self-sabotage, and still others are suffering from an identity crisis and lack of self-worth. Everyone suffers from these challenges, which culminate and are expressed in various ways for each individual, but they are all tied to one thing: conditioned behavior performed from childhood.

But why do we need to cure our inner child?

We have a tendency to be protective and defensive about our early experiences. The reason why inner child healing and reparenting are required is rather straightforward. To be immersed in a rich inner world is to experience pure unconditional love from yourself. To become more empathic, caring, and compassionate is to cultivate a strong feeling of self. Most importantly, we must become emotionally robust and conscientious individuals who are aware of our responses and reactions and do not become gluttons for suffering and averse to our own enjoyment. The fact is, as adults, we have a unique chance to recover and intentionally select another behavior, regardless of everything we have gone through in the past.

What does this have to do with our parents? Are they harmful?

No, not always. Our parents, in an ideal world, are two self-actualized individuals who enable their children to be seen and heard as the unique individuals that they are. Because we live in a civilization that does not achieve conscious awareness, the majority of us are born to unaware parents. Our parents are reproducing the same patterns they saw as children and in their own homes. They operate from their own wounded shadow self since they never mastered the skills for constructively processing their emotions or even the understanding of the necessity to process their emotions.

It is critical to remember that our parents behave only on the basis of their own awareness. We can only give what we have practiced receiving. As a result, playing the blame game is futile and can lead to even more strained relationships with our parents and relatives.

So, what is reparenting, exactly?

Reparenting is the act of providing oneself with what you did not receive as a kid, namely all of the emotional understanding, caring, and love that you needed. You deserved unconditional love and support, but you were pushed to think that love and acceptance had to be won by doing specific things. Perhaps you came to view yourself as undeserving of love if you did not behave in a specific manner or meet the expectations of others. Reparenting is our obligation to ourselves to heal this hurt. That is something we owe ourselves.

When is the best moment to repent, and how can we get started?

As soon as you recognize your difficulties and have identified the source. It is doable for everyone. It takes time, dedication, and a great deal of patience. Every day, you will have to show up for yourself. There are no excuses. There are no shortcuts. There are no short-term remedies. However, it will help you to heal, forgive, and go on. A joyful by-product is being able to have happy, loving, and rewarding relationships, friendships, and companionships.

The Four Pillars of Reparenting

The four pillars of reparenting include:

1. discipline
2. joy
3. emotional regulation
4. self-care

Please be advised, some may be more challenging than others, depending on our life experiences.

Discipline is sometimes the most difficult aspect since we naturally seek comfort, and discipline typically has a bad connotation in our thoughts. Some people find it difficult to experience joy because they believe they do not deserve it, that they must earn it.

This is why we must be patient with ourselves and others, because the end result is a life that is extremely satisfying.

So, to begin, here is how to get started:

1. **Breathe.** Keep in mind that reparenting is a process that will likely extend over days, weeks, or months. Doing too much too rapidly might overwhelm you, causing a reversion to our old habits. Pause and take a deep breath if you sense it becoming too intense or uncomfortable. Take it at your own speed—consistent and comfortable.

2. **Make it a habit to maintain your promises to yourself.** Begin small. Every day, make a commitment to yourself and keep it. It may be as simple as drinking 8 glasses of water, listening to a couple of songs, writing a page in your notebook, or meditating for 10 minutes. Anything that doesn't seem excessive to you. Simply avoid making promises that will take up too much time at first. Anything from a few minutes to a half-hour is OK. If you do this regularly you will see a visible change in terms of reparenting of your inner child.

3. **Believe in someone you can rely on (other than your parents).** Inform the person that you are embarking on this quest. Do not include your parents since it may cause them to feel inadequate as parents. The purpose of reparenting is for you to heal, not for them to feel awful. Inform a friend, partner, or sibling. Any assistance would be greatly appreciated.

4. **Treat yourself.** Consider what you require right now. What can you do to make yourself happy? It may be something as simple as a warm bath, or a massage and spa treatment, or even that snack you crave but don't let yourself enjoy. If you like, you can sunbathe or swim. Alternatively, jump in the puddle while it's pouring rain.

5. **Learn to enjoy yourself.** We will rapidly dismiss the truth that we are showing up for ourselves if we are not recognized, applauded, and seen for the unique individual that we are. It is tough to

reparent ourselves. Recognize the bravery required. Take charge of your progress. Celebrate the person you're becoming.

What is Shadow Work? How This Practice Can Help You Live a Better Life

The "shadow self" refers to components of ourselves that have been pushed down into the unconscious—aspects of ourselves about which we feel concerned, humiliated, or frustrated, and hence repress.

The concept of the shadow self is founded on the idea that we metaphorically bury those aspects of our personalities that we are afraid would not be received, accepted, or appreciated by others; hence, we keep them in the 'shadows.' In a nutshell, our shadow selves are the actual versions of ourselves that we fear displaying to the rest of society.

This is the discipline of accepting what has happened to us, and releasing guilt and judgment so that we can be our authentic selves.

Carl Jung, a Swiss psychologist of the twentieth century, devoted his life to researching the human psyche and mind. Among his many contributions to psychoanalysis was the concept of the "shadow self." The inclusion of the word 'shadow' in this statement may appear eerie at first, but this is nothing to be concerned about!

The shadow self frequently presents itself by leading us to be provoked by another person's words or actions, to suffer inner tension and cognitive dissonance, to criticize or lash out at others, or to feel insecure and held back.

Shadow work is the practice of working with our shadow selves to eliminate the negative impact they have on our lives and to integrate the many aspects of ourselves into one whole.

Over the course of a lifetime, we may have pushed small parts of ourselves so far away that we are unaware of what is hidden in our shadow self, perhaps fearing what we may find hidden away. Shadow work is the bringing to light, processing, and re-acceptance of those small parts—piece by piece and one by one—in order to become a whole, entire, and integrated self.

Shadow work is essentially a type of psychoanalysis (as psychoanalysis is at the core of Jungian psychology). Regardless of the terminology chosen, Jung claimed that integrating the segmented versions of the self is a powerful thing (Kellend, 2015).

What Benefits Does Shadow Work Offer?

While shadow work is not always simple, since it is frequently accompanied by the pain of previous rejection, repairing the schism between the aware and shadow selves may be a life-changing experience. "Shadow labor is the way of the heart warrior," according to Jung (Kellend, 2015).

Jung believed that such a procedure may aid in the development of a balanced existence and a sense of harmony within oneself. Feeling whole, rather than fragmented, may give us a new feeling of freedom, allowing us to see life in new ways and experience things we wouldn't or couldn't previously.

Addressing the emotional baggage that has long been buried in our shadows can help us to show up more fully and consciously for our commitments and relationships in life, whether that's being a better spouse, sister, kid, parent, teacher, mentor, friend, or any of the myriad other roles we serve throughout our lives. In an ever-changing and often restrictive environment, shadow work also helps us to feel stronger sensations of power and personal agency.

Shadow work almost assures more authenticity in everything we do by developing us into the most authentic versions of ourselves that we've ever been.

Finally, by accepting and mending the aspects of ourselves that we've assigned to our shadows, we may learn to express those qualities in healthy ways rather than concealing them until they appear in unhealthy, uncontrollable ways (lashing out at others due to anger, or creating a toxic body image and inner dialogue). This acceptance can then bloom into a strong sense of self-love.

Benefits of Shadow Work for Inner Child Healing

It is critical for your mental health and well-being to have a good relationship with the juvenile aspects of your personality.

Inner child shadow work has been linked to a higher sense of safety, love, support, and creativity in people's lives, according to Lule University's research on health throughout one's lifetime (Cotec, 2020).

Shadow work has also been demonstrated to aid in the treatment of relationship problems and depression, and it may be utilized to improve your ability to discover happiness in your life.

Inner child work can assist your healing in the following ways:

- cultivate your creative and free spirit
- stop emotional outbursts (tantrums/outbursts)
- heal toxic shame and guilt, allowing you to experience more love and support in your relationships
- set and maintain firmer limits
- requests should be made without becoming upset or overreacting
- and many more ways!

In essence, completing inner child work and shadow work, will help you to combine diverse components of your personality into a more solid and whole sense of self.

5 Steps to Healing Your Inner Child Through Shadow Work

Healing means connecting with the child who resides inside you by listening to that part of yourself, and assisting it in expressing repressed feelings. Only when you have processed any hurt or trapped memory will you be able to go forward and nurture a healthy inner child.

These five steps can help you mend your inner child:

1. Recognize the trauma or harmful pattern. The purpose of this initial stage is to bring any suppressed components of your personality to the surface. This initial phase is ideal for shadow work.
2. Investigate the source of the trauma. Consider where the trauma triggered and initially manifested itself. Consider your age, where you were, and what was going on.
3. Travel back in time by using your active imagination. If it feels

comfortable, attempt to return to the time when the initial trauma occurred. Try to observe with the eyes of a caring adult.

4. Encourage your inner kid. Approach your younger self in your recollection for solace and be a supportive ally to yourself. If no one was there for you back then, you are there for your inner child today.

5. Repeat these steps as many times as you like/need. It may take some time to process these intense feelings from your history. Be patient, and simply show up. You will eventually experience a great deal of healing and a stronger connection with your inner child.

Journal Prompts for Inner Child Shadow Work

Writing prompts are another effective technique for investigating the shadow and the inner child. Set up some time for reflection and writing for this exercise.

When responding to these prompts in a diary or notepad, try to write as quickly as possible. With freestyle writing, you're attempting to enter a flow state, allowing your subconscious to surface. Don't bother about editing or spelling—just write.

Here are some writing prompts:

- Do you think you had a decent childhood? How functional was your home life while you were growing up?
- What were your favorite childhood activities? If you gave up any in adulthood, what made you decide to stop?
- What do I miss most about being a child?
- What could I do to increase my sense of fun and creativity?

Shadow work is an excellent approach to experiencing inner healing and transformation, and all that is required is self-awareness. Every person on the planet has gone through a terrible phase in their lives that has left them with shadows. The good news is that the entire cosmos is on our side, attempting to help us heal. Every action in the cosmos is geared toward development and expansion.

We are given several opportunities to confront our shadow selves in order to eventually be free of them. It makes no difference how long you stave off your shadow self. It will continue to appear in your reality unless you pay attention to it.

The fragmented self longs to be reunited, and we will be given opportunities to see pieces of ourselves that we have hidden, rejected, denied, and disowned.

The more you recognize and embrace your shadow self, the more embodied you become as a conscious person, and the more control you will have over yourself and your life.

Key Takeaways

- Look out for the impact of trauma on your emotional and physical health.
- No matter what you have been through in childhood, there's no need to get depressed over the past or question, why me? Instead, reparent yourself so you could break free from the vicious cycle of trauma.
- Shadow work brings out the emotions that you have pushed back in order to help you address them and work accordingly. It is essential to follow the methods of shadow work to gain maximum benefits.

- Don't feel lost while reparenting, following the four steps: discipline, joy, emotional regulation and self-care, at your own speed, will help you.
- Though difficult, embrace the journey to help free yourself from the trauma that's holding you back.

4

Phases of the Healing Process

"Trauma doesn't discriminate and doesn't just happen to "bad" people"

— KRISTIN ANDERSON

This chapter talks about:

- Trauma and recovery stages
- Being your authentic self to win
- The advantages of simply being you
- The personal story of Brené Brown

Trauma and Recovery Stages

These days, we hear a lot about trauma. The news is also rife with horrific events. Trauma does not discriminate and does not only affect 'evil' individuals. Trauma is a human experience that must be understood and treated. But do we truly comprehend the impacts of trauma?

Knowing the phases of trauma might help you heal and feel more in control of what you're going through. Investigate the following steps to become more aware of your recovery process.

Safety and Stabilization

You are likely to retreat as a result of the distressing experience. This retreat process is a form of self-preservation. You are likely to experience rage, guilt, anxiety, and denial during this process. Other emotions may also arise depending on who you are as an individual. It's natural to feel uncomfortable in your own body, in your relationships, and in your surroundings. This stage might span several weeks, months, or even years. This is especially true if the trauma is not processed, acknowledged, and supported throughout therapy.

During the stability and safety stages, begin by assessing your feelings. This is the base to start from because once you find out what you will be working on, it will make the process easier. So, sit back and relax while recalling the trauma. It is easier said than done, but trust the process. This will be the last time you will ever need to recall the trauma, then you will experience the wonders of moving on.

To heal, you must first learn how to manage challenging emotions by developing new coping abilities. Therapists will understand if discussing the trauma is too difficult for you. In this scenario, the therapist may teach you how to settle yourself through mindfulness, yoga, and deep breathing. This period of recuperation should also include the development of new routines.

Mourning and Reminiscence

During this stage, you'll start to come up with your own solutions to the question, "What does it all mean?" This stage of healing is primarily about processing and making sense of the experience. The idea is to create a space where you may reflect on the experience without reliving it. This phase can be completed at your own speed. If you're working with a therapist, they'll continue to prioritize safety and stability. When you are ready, you can lament the losses caused by the traumatic experience. Discuss your feelings. Allow yourself to let go of negative emotions and thoughts. During this period, be kind to yourself. Be patient and empathetic. There is no such thing as a 'correct' time frame.

As mentioned in chapter two, EMDR may also be a useful therapy during this stage. EMDR is a therapy approach that allows you to reflect on a traumatic incident while focusing on bilateral external stimuli. Tapping, buzzing, or eye movements might be the stimulation you need.

Reconnection and Integration

Our sense of ourselves may be distorted following a traumatic occurrence. Because the consequences of the traumatic experience are so severe, it may appear to define us. The final step of trauma rehabilitation assists you in overcoming these consequences so that you can live a full life. You will develop a new sense of self throughout this era. You will also build on positive experiences and start planning for the future. You will have a role in reconnecting with people and redefining important connections.

Taking meaning from pain may be experienced on a smaller scale that is just as powerful. You could opt to live a better lifestyle or change occupations, for example. You empower yourself and others as a result of your efforts. You'll develop new, healthy self-beliefs that will help you to go ahead into your new sense of reality, a reality that is produced by you and that you're motivated to accomplish.

You Are Not Alone: Navigating the Stages of Trauma

Remember that you are never alone in experiencing trauma, even if your reactions and coping techniques differ from those of others. Take the help of a therapist if you need extra help progressing through the phases of trauma. A therapist can help you cope with your trauma in a healthy and helpful way. They can assist you in better understanding yourself and making sense of how you're feeling.

The trauma itself gets ingrained in your past. It no longer defines you, but rather serves as a chapter in your life story. Being able to now fully comprehend the significance of the incident, you are prepared to take action. The goal of this stage is to make use of the traumatic event. For example, you could decide to work with or assist individuals who have been through similar trauma. You may consider publishing a book or giving a public talk on your experience.

Be Your Authentic Self to Win

Still, rather than resorting to external sources, digging within yourself can provide the answers you seek and bring the greatest fulfillment if you ever have the sensation that something is lacking from your life but can't quite put your finger on what it is.

Have you ever been amazed at how a young toddler rushes through life satisfied with no hint of "tone-knowledge?" You were simply yourself when you were younger. You didn't have any other options. Still, when we mature and succumb to the demands imposed by many environments such as education, family, work, or friends, we might sluggishly and unconsciously lose sight of our original tone. Rather, we gradually adapt to what we believe others expect. Finally, we may feel like a fake, a fictitious representation of ourselves that we believe others want to see.

We all put on social masks from time to time. We've all bought into beliefs about what's relevant (and what isn't), and we've all bought into notions of success that aren't ours. They may have originated from our parents, friends, creative organizations, or society as a whole. But we allow these notions to ferment unconsciously in our thoughts, and before long we're crafting a life that conforms to someone else's concept of what a happy life looks like. We're burying our actual passions behind a layer of potential. We lose touch with our true selves. We lose touch with our actual desires and begin to live the life we feel we are meant to or have to live.

Does Being Your True Tone Lead to Loss and Rejection?

Many individuals are concerned that being true to their tone would jeopardize or destroy their security, family, relationships, job, and other vital aspects of their lives. This is simply untrue. When we feel empowered to speak our true tone, rather than losing out, we gain far more than we had ever believed was possible.

What Is Your True Tone?

Your real tone is the "actual you," the person you are after all adaptive masks are removed. Your genuine tone is the person you are when you have a deep inner serenity and awareness. When your values, pretensions, beliefs, words, actions, and public image fit with your specific values, you connect with this state of being. Although it appears to be a straightforward notion, many of us have a difficult time allowing our real tone to take center stage.

How Do You Find Your True Tone?

Consider the following tips when you're ready to investigate and embrace your true tone:

- **Consider a certain force.** A little soul-searching is required to better connect with your real tone. Gather a pen and paper and write a list of the characteristics you admire about yourself. Make another list of the things you like performing and the life consequences that make you happy. What do you enjoy, and why do you enjoy it? This information will be critical in helping you on your journey to finding your unique tone, so take your time assessing your lists.
- **Don't be concerned about what others think.** While it is true that it is easier said than done, you will never be able to be your true tone if you are continually angry over what other people think of you. People-pleasing may appear to be a beneficial attribute, yet pleasing others typically comes at the expense of your own pleasure. Make a vow to quit worrying about being the way other people expect you to be and allow your real tone to show through without making any excuses.

1. *Consider why you care.*
2. *Concentrate on being present in the moment.*
3. *Recognize that most people do not care.*
4. *Practice self-acceptance and love.*
5. *Identify your group of people.*
6. *Recognize that you cannot please everyone.*
7. *Recognize that life is too short.*

- **You should be honored.** The ultimate goal of the journey to becoming your actual tone is to truly appreciate and love oneself. Stop searching for affection and validation from others; no amount of money, love, or renown will fill that gap. If you want to achieve genuine fulfillment in life, you must find and offer yourself love.
- **Accept your fears.** Fear of failing, being judged, disappointing others, or making mistakes is a natural element of human nature, and it may prevent you from being your authentic self. However, the best way to overcome it is to recognize your concerns, appreciate them, and express yourself—go for what you desire. They are, after all, a part of who you are. However, if you're attempting to oppose portions of yourself that you don't like or understand, psychotherapy can assist.

Taking one tiny step at a time is the key to overcoming your worries. Going too quickly or attempting something too frightening before you're ready might backfire.

However, it is equally critical to keep pushing forward. A reasonable level of anxiousness is OK. Don't wait for your nervousness to go away before taking a step forward, or you'll end up waiting for a change that won't occur on its own.

A fear hierarchy made up of modest steps is the best method to construct an action plan. Here's an example of how one could use exposure therapy to overcome their fear of public speaking one step at a time:

1. Talk to yourself in the mirror.
2. Be sure to hold eye contact as you speak.

This is the tried and true method for confronting and overcoming fear. This provides you an edge in recognizing your worries and then working on them to make them your strength.

The Advantages of Simply Being You

When we don't connect with our inner child, we often try to imitate others. However, when we try to imitate them, we lose sight of our purpose. This section goes into detail about this issue and mentions the exercises to help you be yourself and connect with your inner child. Our culture is obsessed with attaining lofty goals, and some may regard taking the time to concentrate on oneself as self-indulgent. Nonetheless, embodying your real tone might produce significantly smaller rewards than other, more tangible career-focused ambitions. I'm not implying that you stop striving for success; rather, it means shifting your emphasis such that the success you accomplish not only yields tangible benefits, but also provides you with a feeling of purpose that is important and rewarding to you.

It's quite satisfying to be comfortable in your own skin. One of the most significant advantages of adopting your real tone is a sense of fulfillment in life that cannot be obtained in any other manner. Indeed, whether your specific relationships or job are in shambles, finding your real tone may help you soar above it all to feel optimistic about your future. Life counseling may help you stay on track as you integrate your views, values, aspirations, and behavior.

Self-control is Essential

Authenticity necessitates discipline. This refers to the ability to execute your principles despite temptations to forsake them. The world of the moment is saturated with glitz, gaudiness, and an emphasis on material gain. As a result, I recommend adopting the following strategies:

- **Reflection about yourself.** The true you necessitates continual tone-reflection. This talent will place you in a state of perfect harmony, leading you to experience less tension since you aren't concerned with another person's point of view, only your own.
- **Visioning.** When you're truly connected to yourself, you might dream about your future tone. Visioning will allow you to feel excited as your fundamental values assist you in raising the bar. The following visioning exercise can help:

  1. *Be sure to sit in a quiet and comfortable place to start visioning.*
  2. *Think about your goals instead of the past and plan to achieve them.*
  3. *Think how your future self will look once you break free from the past.*

- **Translucency.** The fabric of authenticity is woven via open dialogue. When you are certain of who you are and what you stand for, you walk through life with tone-assurance and a sense of inner value.
- **Harkening that is active.** When you're genuine, you notice little emotional stumbling blocks to your pride, which makes you an excellent listener. Because you're secure and at ease in your own skin, it's easier now for you to focus on others.

- **Remember:** If we aren't true to ourselves, we are doing the world, not to mention our families, friends, and visitors, a disservice. Maintain your integrity. Accept your natural tone!
- **Focus.** To be successful in business and at home, you must resist urges and focus on the process until it is complete. Your capacity to adopt your real tone improves your ability to ignore distractions. To increase your focus, you can try the following changes:

1. *Exercise to practice patience.*
2. *Eat a healthy diet, preferably with more fats.*
3. *Get a good night's sleep.*
4. *Make a to-do list to achieve smaller milestones.*

In chapter six, we will dive deeper into becoming the best version of yourself by feeling worthy, authentic, and playful.

Personal Story of Brené Brown

Accepting who we are is a journey that begins with honesty, contemplation, and tone-discovery. Keeping in touch with oneself is a life-long journey. Brené Brown shares her personal revelations (Snowise, 2015):

> I've been there. That pit of confusion where you wonder who the hell you are. Where you wonder if you even actually know yourself at all. I had a moment where I looked in the mirror and stared at myself with almost a foreign level of disconnection. I actually said out loud…"Who am I?" I had lost myself in the chaos and responsibility of modern life. But I was craving to know what made this woman that stood in front of me tick. What did I really want out of life? Standing there staring at myself in the mirror with a feeling of pure confusion was disconcerting to say the least,

but those are the exact moments that you start to wake up to your authenticity. Without having the courage to ask yourself these questions, and have a willingness to delve into yourself and explore, you can never really be in touch with your authentic self. Authenticity requires that you truly connect and know who you are.

Once you've begun to connect with your inner partner and what truly makes you alive, you must maintain that connection, which requires regular practice and dedication. The current world is hectic, frantic, and noisy. When we don't have that established connection with ourselves, it's easy to get caught up in it and washed away.

Key Takeaways

- Remember that you are not alone in the healing process, so don't put too much pressure on yourself. Following the above mentioned steps will guide you in the process.
- Learning to be authentic might require a lot of guts. When you do, though, you liberate yourself and begin to develop a life that provides you joy and significance. You won't get there overnight, but you can get there.
- Once you have accepted your past and start working on it, no one can stop the change you are about to achieve.

5

Letting Go of The Past

*"Every time your fear is invited up, every time you recognize it
and smile at it, your fear will lose some of its strength"*

— THICH NHAT HANH

This chapter talks about:

- Letting go of the past
- How to handle fear and anxiety
- Self-apologies: healing shame and guilt with self-forgiveness
- How do I practice self-forgiveness?

Let Go of the Past

Most of us have been subjected to some type of trauma during our lives. We may have had "big trauma" such as abuse, major loss, or a life-threatening incident, but we may have examples of "small trauma" from situations that were not life-threatening but caused emotional anguish and impacted our way of viewing ourselves, other people, and the world.

Childhood trauma of any form may have an impact on our relationships as well as our mental and physical health. The necessity of making meaning of the trauma, regardless of when it occurred or what form it took, cannot be stressed enough.

This is due to the fact that unresolved trauma may haunt us in ways that resolved trauma does not. According to research, when we fail to handle both big and small traumas, we might become imprisoned in our suffering. Our trauma might have unanticipated consequences in our life (Firestone, 2022). It might make us feel worried and triggered for reasons we don't understand at times.

Unresolved trauma occurs when we do not process it immediately after it occurs or when we do not process it at all. Taking a deep dive into our own narrative may thus do a lot of good.

So, what measures can we take to bring our memories to the surface and comprehend our trauma? Here are nine recommendations I make when assisting folks in developing a cohesive story around their experience:

Watch Out for Exaggerations

To begin, we might seek out locations where we have strong emotional ties. Anything from our partner's tone to a baby's cry might set off feelings associated with prior trauma. When we have a heightened emotional reaction that doesn't seem to suit the situation, we should consider whether there is underlying, unresolved trauma affecting us.

Interpersonal neurobiologist, Daniel Siegel, describes a strategy for acquiring insight into our interior state using the acronym SIFT (sensations, images, thoughts, and feelings). First, we can examine any physical symptoms we may be experiencing, such as our heart pounding or our forehead becoming heated. Then, we may evaluate the images that come to mind. This may be anything from a harsh expression on someone's face to a specific piece of wallpaper in a room. We can then focus on any emotions that occur, such as terror, grief, embarrassment, or rage.

Finally, we can make a mental note of any thoughts that arise, such as, *You should get out of here.* In this circumstance, you are not safe (Siegel, n.d.). The sensations, ideas, sentiments, and thoughts evoked may have more to do with the past than with the present. As a result, they provide insight into events or circumstances that may have been distressing to us at a time when we were unable to completely digest the experience.

Immediately Write Out Ten Childhood Traumas You've Endured

Many people who I invite to participate in this exercise begin by stating, "I don't believe I can think of ten traumas that occurred in my early childhood." Others have felt confident in continuing with a considerably larger list. However, starting with ten generally motivates us to expand our brains and memory and delve into situations and events that we may not initially categorize as trauma. These might be "capital T" or "small t" events.

We frequently try to bury or brush over negative things that happened to us, especially if they were terrifying or occurred while we were too young to properly comprehend them. We may never have recounted our own tales about these occurrences, so we don't frequently remember them. As difficult as it may be at first, identifying the events that have influenced us is beneficial. Even things that have had a significant impact on us that we've disregarded or forgotten. Bringing them to light is the first step toward understanding our narrative.

Give it Some Thought

Certain sections of the tale will make little sense to us when we jot down particular occurrences. We may become aware that many portions of our experience remain unsolved or have slipped from our consciousness. We may detect a muddled timeline or memory gaps. Alternatively, we may reconsider a portion of our tale that we previously viewed in one manner but now see in a completely different light.

Many folks I've spoken with blame themselves as youngsters. For example, one lady grew up believing she had murdered her dog when he was hit by a car after she had unintentionally left her back door open.

As we investigate our memories, it is helpful to identify areas where the tale is disjointed and may benefit from greater contemplation.

Use the RAIN Method to Calm Down

Examining our emotions and recollections may be upsetting. When something unpleasant or stressful occurs, psychologists Jack Kornfield and Tara Brach, advocate the RAIN Approach, which consists of the following four steps:

- **Recognize** the trauma or loss. Take time to consider how you're feeling.
- **Allow/Recognize/Accept** whatever powerful feeling is present in

the moment. We can recognize that this trauma occurred and that it may not be addressed.

- **Investigate** the experience in relation to your history and present life.
- **Nurturing non-identification** with the experience implies that you should not over-identify with what happened or let it define you. Remember that the recollection isn't occurring to you right now and has nothing to do with who you are.

Collect Information

When we have gaps in our recollection, it might be beneficial to ask others to provide their perspectives. Family members and friends who were present at the time of our trauma may be able to provide us with a more complete knowledge of the event. However, there's the potential for an individual close to the situation to disagree with or dismiss our observations, especially if they're puzzled about an occurrence.

In these instances, it's crucial to realize that what the event meant to us is still significant. It's alright to admit that our experience or personal truth influenced our life if it seems real to us. Even still, the advice of someone we trust can help us piece together items we can't recall or have reservations about.

Feel the Full Extent of What Occurred

When we tell our tale, it is certain to elicit strong emotions. Accept that your feelings are genuine and that they matter rather than trying to justify them away.

Allowing ourselves to completely experience the emotion without judgment or attempts to stop it, is a vital step in processing and overcoming the initial trauma. This will provide us with relief.

Remember that our emotions may be like a wave, rising and falling, finally returning us to a state of peace, but only if we allow them to run their complete course.

Make a Note of it

We may continue to write our tales as they come to the surface. In many circumstances, simply writing about them may be really beneficial. Feelings, ideas, and recollections of any kind are allowed.

We must approach the intricacies of our tale with patience, compassion, and without judgment. It can also be helpful to write down what we believe happened based on our present feelings.

When people begin to do this, their memories frequently come to the surface.

Share Your Experience With Someone

Choose someone you can trust and tell them about your trauma. Others may be able to perceive the issue more objectively and contribute fresh insight. Those close to us frequently have a softer attitude and more sympathy for us than we have for ourselves. This can help us understand what happened and improve our attitude toward ourselves. It can assist us in beginning to confront any long-held negative views we've held about ourselves that have arisen as a result of the traumatic incident.

Construct a Logical Story

After we've begun to identify the traumas that occurred, we might ask, "What's a story that makes sense around that trauma?" Even though the facts themselves are nonsensical, we may begin crafting our story in a coherent fashion in which the events make sense to us.

We might begin to feel less fractured inside when we digest what happened in a cohesive manner. We may come to see how we were innocent in particular situations or how specific events affected us far more than we realized. We may approach our situation with compassion and love, just as we would if a friend told us the same tale.

We can feel more connected when we face and share our narrative in a holistic way. By acquiring crucial insight into our triggers and emotions, we may begin to reclaim the sense of peace that our trauma had previously robbed us of. We may stop blaming ourselves for bad things that have happened to us and start seeing ourselves in a different perspective.

How to Handle Fear and Anxiety

This section discusses what you can do on your own to manage fear and anxiety. There are options, approaches, and techniques available to work on your fear and anxiety that add to the work of professionals. These are critical for persons who have been traumatized or who are experiencing acute dread or anxiety.

Avoid Evasion

The only way to overcome fear is to confront it. Avoiding our concerns simply keeps us from progressing—it makes us uneasy. However, be careful with yourself and just do what seems safe to you! If you sense yourself becoming increasingly panicked, take a pause and look for anything pleasant or reassuring to observe or do. When the feeling passes, you can revisit your phobia, taking breaks as required. If you find it difficult to handle persistent concerns or anxieties on your own, keep in mind that therapists may be quite helpful in working through avoidance methods with you. Working with a therapist to provide a secure setting where you may face your anxiety and recreate your memories is especially crucial if you have suffered trauma.

You can attempt mindfulness meditation if your fear or anxiety is milder. All you have to do is sit quietly and pay attention to the current moment and try to recognize any feelings of dread or worry that occur. Be as inquisitive as you possibly can. Take note of the worry. Take note of how it feels in your body. Take note of any linked ideas. See if you can just observe it as it is; don't get caught up in the tale or try to get rid of or modify it.

And, if necessary, take a pause and focus your attention on something neutral, such as your breath or your hands on your lap. It's worth noting that if you're feeling too upset to be interested, it's best to take a break, open your eyes, and examine what's around you, or go for a short stroll.

Encourage Positivism

Fear encourages us to notice and recall bad occurrences, which confirms our impression that the world is a terrible place. We may attempt to alter that by consciously observing what is positive—the joy we experience when we see someone we care about, the pleasure of a bright day, the beauty in nature, the fun of a trip, the humor in a scenario.

According to Barbara Fredrickson's research, optimism broadens our perspective—we physically have a larger vision, which provides us with more possibilities (Fredrickson, 2014). The more we practice positively, the stronger it becomes, allowing us to operate even in challenging situations.

Look for Significance

Fear has the power to disrupt our perception of the world as we know it. Those who have undergone trauma may have also suffered significant losses, leading them to question the meaning of their existence. Trauma survivors frequently feel guilty about what happened, believing, illogically, that they might have stopped it in some way, and this shame can add to worries about their significance.

However, whether we are suffering from anxiety or trauma, it is critical to re-establish a sense of purpose. An 80-year study of variables that influence lifespan, discovered that those who return to healthy habits after trauma are the ones who can find purpose in the terrible event and rebuild a feeling of security in the world (Delagran, n.d.).

Meaningful Therapy for Healing

Logotherapy, which literally means "healing by meaning," has been shown to be effective in treating people suffering from post-traumatic stress disorder (PTSD).

Part of the success of this treatment stems from just allowing people to speak their stories and feel understood, which aids in the healing process. Another aspect is determining how to put talents and experience, particularly those gained through trauma, to use in a meaningful way. For example, a person who has suffered from PTSD because of childhood trauma, may find purpose in assisting others who have suffered similar trauma.

Seek Assistance

Fear might sometimes make us feel estranged from others. The longevity experiment also discovered that the strength of one's social interactions was a crucial predictor of lifespan among persons who had experienced trauma in their lives (Delagran, n.d.).

This is due to a variety of factors. Friends and relatives can assist us in making an accurate evaluation of the hazard. We are more confident in our ability to deal with problems when we have the support of others. In addition, having a loved one around relaxes us and decreases our fight or flight response.

Embrace the Nature

Being in nature decreases fear and anxiety while increasing pleasant sensations, as evidenced by the emerging area of nature-based treatments. People express their sentiments when they see a scene of natural beauty using terms like peace, beauty, happiness, hope, and aliveness. Being linked to nature not only improves people's mental well-being, but it also lowers blood pressure, heart rate, muscular tension, and the creation of stress hormones—all of which are signs of worry and fear.

So, if you're experiencing sensations of fear or anxiety, go for a walk or run in a park or greenspace. Physical activity will improve your mood in addition to the healing effects of nature.

Self-Compassion Should be Practiced

Many members of racial, sexual, ethnic, and gender minority groups suffer greater levels of dread and anxiety as a result of estrangement and discrimination, which occasionally involves violence, according to research and personal testimonies (Robinson & Segal, 2018). For persons who are facing this sort of chronic threat, self-compassion may be a profoundly therapeutic practice. That's because, in addition to treating oneself as you would a loving friend, self-compassion entails contemplating the shared suffering of others like you.

Face your concerns and anxieties so that they do not become crippling. Determine how you may gain a sense of personal control or mastery over your life. Finally, even if you are plagued with worry, don't neglect other aspects of your life. Even when working towards greater security, it is possible to find happiness in relationships and a sense of purpose.

Consider yourself as a child. Think back to a time when you were feeling vulnerable, when you were being treated harshly, or when you were in emotional distress and needed to be consoled. Take note of any emotions that arise. Some people find it beneficial to look at a photograph of themselves when they were younger. Consider how you would care for that child in a hypothetical situation. What do you think you'd say to him or her? What would you do to comfort this child? Once you answer these questions, you will feel greater relaxation and content in your life.

Self-Apologies: Healing Shame and Guilt with Self-Forgiveness

We often hear how important it is to forgive people who have wronged us, but what about forgiving ourselves? Is it also important? Absolutely. When we injure others, we feel remorse and apologize. However, we frequently punish ourselves for mistakes and create negative self-images as a result. These sensations are accompanied by emotions of shame and guilt. While these sentiments are comparable and can occur concurrently, they are slightly distinct.

Guilt and Shame

Shame and guilt can seem extremely similar in that they both make us feel horrible about ourselves. However, guilt may be defined as being dissatisfied with oneself for breaching an essential internal value or rule of behavior. Feeling guilty can be beneficial since it can lead to good behavioral change. With shame, one may also experience self-dissatisfaction, but no value has been violated. We feel guilty when we feel horrible about anything we did or didn't do. When we are ashamed, we feel horrible about ourselves. When we feel guilty, we must realize that it is OK to make errors. When we feel ashamed, we must understand that it is alright to be ourselves.

Shame refers to feeling bad about a certain feature of your body and then comparing it to others, thus making you feel more judgmental about yourself. Over time, this feeling becomes deeply entrenched within. Thus, when you feel ashamed of your trauma or something you did not do. This affects your adult mindset and behavior.

Shame is harmful because it leads to poor self-esteem (feelings of unworthiness) and behaviors that perpetuate a negative self-image. Shame may lead to self-criticism, blame, neglect, self-destructive actions, self-sabotaging behaviors, the sense that you don't deserve wonderful things, and rage, among other emotions.

Self-Forgiveness

So, how do we lessen our feelings of shame and guilt? Forgiveness of oneself, especially when it comes to humiliation, is key. Self-forgiveness promotes emotional stability and mental tranquility. The more guilt you are able to repair, the more clearly you will be able to see yourself—the good and the troubled. You will be able to identify and acknowledge to yourself and others how you have injured them. Compassion is the cure to embarrassment. Self-compassion works to neutralize guilt and eliminate the poisons that shame creates. Self-forgiveness is an essential component of self-compassion. It relieves the agony produced by shame in our body, mind, and soul, and it aids in the entire healing process.

How Do I Practice Self-Forgiveness?

Self-Understanding

Understanding the events, traumas, and pressures that have led to the formation of harmful thinking patterns in your life can go a long way toward forgiving yourself for the ways you have harmed yourself and/or others. Understanding the reasons behind your coping mechanisms or beliefs might help you avoid blaming yourself for decisions you may or may not have made.

According to research, the long-term impacts of trauma are most visible and noticeable when people are agitated, in unfamiliar settings, or in scenarios that remind them of the circumstances of their trauma. As a result, events might sometimes elicit emotions that we wish we didn't have. Understanding oneself via healthy coping skills, counseling, and support, on the other hand, may significantly increase your ability to forgive and move forward.

Compassion for Oneself and Common Humanity

Kristin Neff, is regarded as a pioneer in the subject of self-compassion. The second key ingredient of self-compassion, according to her conception, is acknowledgment of the universal human experience—or what she refers to as "Common Humanity." She writes in her book, *Self-Compassion*, that "self-compassion recognizes the truth that all human beings are imperfect, that bad decisions and feelings of regret are unavoidable" (Self Apologies, 2021).

We've all committed errors. Knowing this and realizing you are not alone, might help you feel compassion to forgive yourself. Compassion for yourself does not absolve you of responsibility for your actions, but it can liberate you from negative self-talk that keeps you from forgiving yourself, allowing you to respond to the situation with clarity.

When you evaluate your errors, it becomes evident that you did not deliberately choose to do them, and even when you did, the rationale for your actions was tinted by previous traumas. Specific patterns emerged as a result of the guilt you carried, outside situations, and extra pressures. These external influences might include genetics, family history, and living conditions.

"When we begin to see that we are a product of innumerable influences, we don't need to take our 'personal faults' so personally," Kristin Neff states in *Self-Compassion* (Self Apologies, 2021). We might be less judgemental of ourselves and others when we recognize the complicated web of conditions in which we are all enmeshed. A thorough awareness of interconnection enables us to feel compassion for the reality that we're doing the best we can with the hand life has dealt us (Self Apologies, 2021).

Having to Earn Your Forgiveness

If you are having difficulty engaging in self-forgiveness, be open and inquire with yourself. "Why wouldn't I want to forgive myself?" you might ask. If you say, "I don't deserve it" that's your shame speaking. If you still believe you don't deserve forgiveness, you may believe you must earn it.

What steps do you take to earn forgiveness? Be honest about what you believe you require forgiveness for and what you believe you have done, as this may help you to alter some negative ideas and be more compassionate and forgiving of yourself.

Write a letter to the person who you want to forgive (in this case yourself). In this letter you'll write about what you want to forgive yourself for and why. After it is written, you will burn it, and leave it behind.

Your Inner Child and Soft Boundaries

Assume you grew up believing you were unloved. As a result, whether consciously or subconsciously, you will spend your entire life yearning for love, thinking: *I need to be a nice girl or a good guy; and in order to feel loved, I must not ever say no.* And so you wind up giving and giving to the point of contempt because saying no is something you find really difficult to do.

Your Inner Child and Rigid Boundaries

Assume you grew up witnessing your mother or father struggle to say no, and you saw what this lack of boundaries caused them, or perhaps to both of you. So, as a youngster, you make a promise to yourself that you will never allow anyone to get too close to you and that you will never let your guard down. From that perspective, you create hard boundaries, believing that you must protect yourself by erecting those walls, and that if you don't, you will suffer in the same way that others close to you have suffered.

The reason that limits are set in both situations is because they are ego-based reactions. Because of a painful event, the ego protects you by establishing these limits. It ultimately backfires.

So, what steps can you take to remedy the desire to set rigid boundaries?

Step 1: Let Go of Your Grip on the Agony

There is a need to defend oneself if the ego is involved. Because your inner child did not feel secure and was injured, the ego made agreements and limits to help your inner child feel comfortable. If you let go of your grief, you will behave and react from a place of neutrality rather than anguish. To let go of agony:

- **Write.** Writing is a therapy for almost all of the issues out there. So make sure to write it all out so there is nothing holding you back.
- **Grow your creativity.** Drawing, knitting, painting, dancing, photography, music, ceramics, or any other hobby that you like is acceptable. This practice is comparable to journal writing in that it allows for the discharge of emotions.
- **Divert your attention to something else**. Our emotional condition can become overpowering and difficult to regulate at times. This is when having a diversion might help you cope. A diversion might be as easy as watching a movie or going out for coffee with a buddy.
- **Exercise**. Physical activity is an important component of mind-body wellbeing. Movement can help our unpleasant emotions get unstuck, allowing us to process and release them.
- **Eliminate unhealthy thinking patterns**. Learn to recognize harmful habits of thought, such as rumination or negative thinking, and attempt to change such patterns. This is a frequent cognitive-behavioral method used to treat stress, as well as depression and trauma. For example, if you see yourself indulging in negative thinking or obsessing on a traumatic scenario, utilize self-talk to break the cycle. You might tell yourself, "I will get through this," "I am strong," or "I am bold."

Step 2– Act From a Place of Loving Neutrality

Once you've let go of the fear and given yourself what you need, you'll be in a better position to see and comprehend that other people have their own things going on as well—their own filters and viewpoints through which they see and live. They, too, frequently behave or respond depending on their own experiences. With that in mind, act, respond, and make decisions from a neutral, loving place.

This neutrality becomes simpler to maintain as you have a better understanding of others' point of view. When you approach the world and those around you with loving neutrality, no matter what life throws at you, you help bring clarity and healing to all involved, including yourself. There will be no need for hard boundaries.

Step 3– Positively Express Yourself

Even if you're dealing with a challenging or unfavorable situation, it's necessary to express yourself. But you must do so in a productive and respectful manner.

Don't be scared to stand up for yourself and confront those who question you and/or your rights. You may even allow yourself to get irritated! But remember to keep your emotions under check and to be courteous at all times.

Key Takeaways

- Childhood trauma may have an impact on our adult relationships as well as our mental and physical health.
- Trauma remains unresolved if we do not face it.

- Creating an unified story entails admitting our mistakes, sharing our stories, and feeling the agony of our trauma.
- Use stress-reduction practices like mindfulness, meditation, or cardiovascular exercise to help you relax.
- Refocus your attention on the pleasant emotions you experience on a regular basis.
- Work to discover your life's meaning and purpose.

6

Feeling Worthy, Authentic, and Playful: Becoming Your Best Self

"It takes a very long time to become young"

— PABLO PICASSO

This chapter talks about:

- 8 easy ways to release your inner child's creativity
- Inner child vs. inner critic: a creative fight
- Reparent your inner child to improve your self-esteem and live a happier life
- Parenting with intention
- 5 ways to live your best life

8 Easy Ways to Release Your Inner Child's Creativity

The joy of childhood play is an excellent source of inspiration for adult creativity.

Do You Need a Creative Outlet?

Perhaps your day job entails arranging Excel sheets as your most creative task. Perhaps being creative is your day job, and you're exhausted by the continual need to come up with new ideas.

Whether you're a full-time creative or don't have a creative bone in your body, having a creative outlet aside from your day-to-day work is important.

Why is Having a Creative Outlet so Important?

We have an intrinsic drive to express ourselves as humans. We require a means to express our feelings and experiences, which allows us to deal with our everyday lives and comprehend the world around us. Simply discussing our difficulties isn't enough. We require a creative retreat to assist us in connecting with ourselves on a deeper level.

Furthermore, there are scientific studies that corroborate the multiple benefits of creativity. It can help reduce stress and anxiety, enhance physical and mental health, and increase IQ (Chen, 2020; Robinson, 2021). Fortunately, there are several methods for releasing your creativity. And you don't have to be Picasso or Mozart to benefit. In fact, you probably already know how to perform a number of activities since you did them as a youngster.

Here are some ideas for making time for yourself and maintaining a creative outlet.

Things to consider while looking for a creative outlet:

- **Have a sense of humor.** As adults, we are often too focused on attaining positive outcomes. We'll quit a creative project if we don't excel at it quickly. Allow yourself to be surprised when it comes to finding a creative expression. Consider when you were a child and doodled or played make-believe. Attempt to channel that sense of enjoyment and enjoy the process.
- **Have some structure.** Is it possible to have fun while following the rules? Yes! Structure and regularity will really assist you in connecting with your creative side. There's a reason why writers are overwhelmed by the blank page: the sensation of possibilities may be overpowering.

1. *Try setting up a regular day and time to engage in creative pursuits, whatever they may be.*
2. *If you're just getting started with creative writing, try keeping a word prompt diary. Instead of feeling obligated to create anything from scratch, you may utilize the word prompt as a jumping-off point for brainstorming ideas.*

Suggestions to Be Creative

- **Adult coloring books** - For good reason, adult coloring books are a popular creative activity. Coloring has been shown in studies to reduce stress and anxiety. Coloring enables you to get out of your thoughts and concentrate on the subject at hand. We spend so much of our adult lives problem-solving, evaluating, and juggling job and home life. Coloring allows our minds to rest and be inspired by the colors on a page, taking a break from all of the thinking and fretting.

- **Watercolors** - You may get started straight away by purchasing inexpensive paints and brushes. Smooth paint brush strokes and a soothing palette of water colors are so pleasant and relaxing.
- **Dance class** - Getting in touch with your physical side is the best way to get out of your thoughts. Try a salsa or flamenco class, or any other activity that allows you to express yourself through dance. Because it helps you to connect with your physical body, a dance class might be especially beneficial if your profession demands you to write and communicate all day.
- **Make a collage** - Create a physical Pinterest board by gathering periodicals and catalogs and clipping out any image that speaks to you. Maybe you'll make a vision or inspiration board – go with your gut and see what you come up with. These graphics may be glued to a paper or pinned to a corkboard.
- **Build with Legos** - Legos, like adult coloring books, are making a resurgence as adult sets. Allow your imagination to soar as you construct vast universes one brick at a time.
- **Cook a dinner** - Being creative does not require you to learn a new instrument or write a poem. In fact, when you're inspired by ingredients and flavors, creating a meal can be a creative endeavor. Furthermore, the physical sensations of cutting, dicing, and stirring are guaranteed to be a terrific stress reliever, and the ingestion of flavors and fragrances will alert the senses, making you more susceptible to creative thoughts.
- **Playing instruments** - Playing instruments is beneficial to your health and creativity. They might help you relax and enter a meditative state, and learning different instruments is a great way to relieve tension! If you've grown weary of crunching statistics or staring at text all day, take an instrument lesson or simply get a bongo to pound on at home while listening to music.
- **Solve riddles** - If music and dancing aren't your thing, perhaps

board games and puzzles are. Make some tea and get out a puzzle. And by fitting the puzzle pieces together, you might just be able to see the greater picture–not just on the board, but also in your own life!

Remember that the simpler the creative activity, the better. Consider the things you enjoyed as a youngster, the pure thrill of doing something enjoyable that engages your imagination is what childhood enjoyment is all about.

We hope you discover a creative outlet that is both soothing and pleasant, whether you're building a collage or coloring in a book.

Inner Child vs. Inner Critic: A Creative Fight

Adults mourn their childhood's pure curiosity, and artists attempt to recover their lost childish inventiveness. The creative process might feel like a never-ending conflict between an inner child and an inner critic. Can this creative conflict be resolved in favor of creative balance?

Getting Older

Being a youngster is synonymous with being inquisitive. It seems as though children ask 107 questions each hour. However, as we become older, we begin to accumulate factual information, practical shortcuts, and mental models to help us make faster judgments. In a society that values speed as a metric of performance, we seek the shortest road to our objectives. We place so much emphasis on understanding *how* quickly we can arrive at a desired end that we neglect to pause and ask *why* along the way.

And when we do ask ourselves questions, we are frequently motivated by self-doubt. Is my labor sufficient? What will the public think? Our inner critic is trained by a learning system that emphasizes getting the right answer and outperforming others on prescribed assignments. Listening to our inner critic may lead to conformist work rather than superior creative work.

While the inner child has typically been employed in psychology to represent an unconscious archetype pointing to unresolved childhood events, it may be welcomed to help us better balance our creativity. In his book, *Psychotherapy for the Soul*, psychologist Stephen Diamond asks, "Has your adult self spent time with your inner child today?" (Diamond, 2008).

Retraining the Inner Critic

We frequently discuss silencing our inner critic. Connecting with your inner child and releasing your youthful creativity does not mean we need to quiet our inner critic. Instead, it's about retraining how the inner critic interacts with the inner child: unlearning self-doubt, pointless competitiveness, and dread of failure.

As with many unfavorable emotional experiences, accepting the voice within might help us better comprehend it. Turning self-criticism into self-reflection may boost your creativity by allowing you to go deeper into your own mind and confront your ideas and feelings in a healthy manner. We disarm the inner critic with love rather than violence.

So, how do you go about doing so? Positive self-talk is a simple technique for transforming self-criticism into self-reflection. For instance, positive self-talk appears to assist athletes enhance both their performance and their mental condition. A meta-analysis of 32 studies on the subject backs up these claims (Diamond, 2008).

There are easy steps you may take to make room for positive self-talk:

- **Create your own fun.** Integrate playfulness into your creative work as a discipline. Talk yourself into doing new things, let go of the aim, and surround yourself with people who are fun to be around.
- **Accept JOMO (Joy of Missing Out).** It's fine to forgo an adult event in order to spend time with your inner kid at home. Do you want to sketch, write poems, or learn how to 3D print instead of going out for drinks with your coworkers? Proceed with caution. Feel the thrill of missing out.
- **Inquire why**. Don't allow your lack of apparent expertise keep you from asking questions. Continue to ask why, as if you were a child. Train your inner critic to convert self-doubt into exploratory inquiries.

Over time, your inner critic transforms into your inner coach. Instead of it being a paralyzing fight that stifles your creative process, it propels your personal progress. *What would others think?* becomes instead, *Who could provide me constructive feedback?* and *Does it feel good enough?* based upon societal criteria, we ask ourselves, *Does it feel pleasant?* based on our own feeling of play and curiosity.

"It is never too late to have a good childhood," Tom Robbins wrote. It is never too late to make amends. Kill your inner critic with love so that it becomes your inner coach, and embrace your inner child's fun and curiosity to boost your creativity. Your inner dialogues will be a lot more joyful, and this will be reflected in your life and job (Diamond,

2008).

Heal Your Inner Child to Improve Your Self-Esteem and Live a Happier Life!

As mentioned before, reparenting is an effective method for healing childhood emotional traumas. In essence, you become the parent you lacked as a child. And, by providing to yourself what you did not receive as a child, you are liberated from the past.

This is also critical for developing self-esteem and mending emotional traumas from the past. As a consequence, you will be able to have good relationships and live a happy life.

Childhood Adversity

Sometimes parents fail to offer the psychological, emotional, and physical support necessary for a child's healthy growth. Adults who are stuck in their prior trauma might be dominated by their wounded inner child indefinitely.

And this may lead to bad adult decisions, particularly when it comes to relationships and creating appropriate boundaries. Because you were unable to build a strong sense of self as a youngster, emotional or physical abuse will have an impact on your future judgment. As a consequence, you may be unsure of how to establish healthy limits with others. Regrettably, this may lead to a lot of heartache, stress, and drama later in life.

Hurting Words

If you're harboring childhood scars as an adult, there are very genuine and, sadly, frequent causes for this. Your parents may have tried to teach and protect you, but they may have really done the opposite. The following are some of the most typical ways that children's feelings are rejected or minimized:

- You were made to feel bad for expressing your feelings.
- You were yelled at.
- You were penalized for attempting to speak out or express your uniqueness.
- You were humiliated by your parents or other family members.
- You were subjected to criticism or verbal assaults.
- You were raised to believe that you were responsible for your parents' unhappiness.
- You were dragged into grownup topics and discussions.
- You were taught that having your own ideas is unacceptable.
- You did not get proper physical attention, such as hugs, kisses, or cuddles.
- Your emotions were not validated or given any weight.
- You were physically disciplined with spankings, slaps, pinches, and other forms of corporal punishment.

So, if you were unwanted as a child or were mentally/physically mistreated or neglected, you most likely have poor self-esteem since you never learned how to connect with yourself.

Then vs. Now

You might be asking yourself why this is so significant. Some people are still unknowingly affected or governed by their unconscious inner child. This is because they lack a true connection to themselves.

As a result, they are unable to attract good partnerships into their life. Childhood trauma causes these harmful and self-destructive behavioral habits.

It also explains why you can be apprehensive, fearful, or insecure. That, however, is not your fault. How else could you feel when you were a youngster and never had adequate safety or mental shelter? And it is for this reason that you must now reparent your inner child in order to mend your life and make good changes!

Taking a Look Outside Yourself

Unfortunately, when your parents do not affirm you or teach you the value of your feelings, you are trained to believe the same. You can't care for yourself or establish self-esteem if you don't appreciate your own feelings. As a result, you evolve into adulthood without knowing you have a self to care for.

When you don't have enough self-confidence, you're taught to ignore your feelings in order to please others. So you search outside of yourself for everything you should be offering to yourself: love, approval, self-esteem, validation. Only when things go really terrible, or you've reached your emotional rock bottom, will you begin to look inside because there's nowhere else to turn.

Parenting with Intention

You can heal your inner child no matter what has happened to you. So, try these activities to accept and strengthen your inner child and become a joyful, healthy adult.

Identify Your Inner Child

When you are hurt as a kid, it is all too common for you to become codependent. This implies that you seek recognition, validation, and affection from sources other than yourself. As a result, the world may become perplexing, if not frightening.

- Maintain an open mind.
- Seek advice from someone younger, most often a child.
- Try going over your childhood recollections, both happy and sad. It can help to make a timeline and write these moments down.
- As a child, take pleasure in the simple things.
- Speak with your inner kid.

Make Use of the Present Moment

You may ground yourself in the present moment by living in the now, not stressing about the future or focusing on the past. Every minute of the day is a new chance to be unconditionally loving, caring, and kind to yourself. And this is just what your inner kid requires to grow and thrive. You may be the attentive parent you wished you had as a child by taking care of yourself.

Self-Care

Self-care is a powerful method for connecting with your inner self. This is a profoundly restorative activity that has the potential to transform the path of your life. Nobody understands what you require better than you.

So, ask yourself, *What brings me joy?* Then do whatever it is that brings you joy. Instead of looking outside of yourself, change your attention and learn to rely on yourself! Consider yourself to be a tiny child. Then, acknowledge your inner being, which is constantly with you. Speak with her (or him). Find out exactly what they require from you.

You are the only one who has the ability to cure your wounds. So, offer your inner child what you wished for as a youngster but did not get. Throughout the day, check in with yourself frequently, by exploring, *How do I feel about this emotion/situation/event?* And then cultivate those emotions.

Recognize Your Inner Child's Requirements

Based on our unique experiences, we all have distinct demands. As a result, everyone's reparenting experience will be unique. This means setting limits, making time for yourself, and being gentle with yourself during the process.

Reparenting is "simply self care," according to Dr. LePera, creator of the "Holistic Psychologist" website. In other words, the idea of reparenting your inner child is predicated on the assumption that you are capable of meeting your own needs. "It's making choices every day in your own best interest." She continues, "It is about becoming conscious of your habits and actions, particularly why you do what you do" (Estrada, 2019).

Parental Reflection

When you are young, the adults who raise you, teach you about yourself. This occurs as a result of parental mirroring.

"Parental mirroring" is defined as a caregiver's ability to precisely reflect a child's expressed thoughts and feelings. And the child's perception of acceptance and validity will be enhanced as a result of this affirmation that he or she has been heard.

As a result, in order to reparent your inner child, you must first supply him/her with what she needed to hear as a youngster. Here are a few major examples of words of healing that your inner child needs to hear:

- I adore you.
- I understand.
- You are flawless and complete.
- You did not deserve it.
- That must have been a really tough situation for you.
- I'm very sorry for what happened to you.
- You are astute.
- You gave it your all.

Visualization of the Inner Child

The following practice can be utilized to heal your inner child:

- Take a seat or lie down in a comfortable, peaceful location.

- Pay attention to your breathing.
- Take slow, deep breaths in and softly exhale. If you notice any stiffness in your body, concentrate on it and breathe into it.
- Exhale to let go of the stress. Continue to take slow, deep breaths in and out.
- Allow your mind to relax and simply accept whatever feelings occur.
- When old hurtful emotions come to the surface, pause and take several deep breaths.
- Imagine a brilliant light streaming through your body, bringing you back to a state of tranquility.

Repeat this practice as soon as you feel responsive and ready.

Love as a Healer

The most powerful healing force in the universe is love. And love has the power to heal even the most profound childhood traumas and grief.

You can choose to consider different ideas and make new decisions when in peaceful contemplation. You will cultivate loving feelings of forgiveness and compassion as you reparent your inner child. This will offer up new avenues for you to cultivate better, happier connections.

True maturity is dependent on recognizing, embracing, and accepting responsibility for loving and raising one's own inner child. And only you have the ability to make positive changes by reconnecting with yourself, increasing your self-esteem, and your confidence. This is an efficient and healthful method to begin making great changes right away!

5 Ways to Live Your Best Life

In the midst of a pandemic that has undeniably aged us all, the urge to embrace our inner child is all the more pressing. We may learn a lot from youngsters, such as their curious, fearless, and carefree attitude toward life. With bills to pay, money to save, errands to do, and a life full of rules and obligations, it's all too easy to lose sight of our curiosity for life and excitement for each day.

That doesn't mean we can't restore those characteristics. Getting in touch with your inner kid is a terrific approach to de-stress and rediscover the creativity and vigor that you had as a youngster and that you still have deep within.

"We get caught up in the grown-up trap and forget to have fun; embracing your inner child can reconnect you with the contentment and simplicity you once experienced as a child," says Nicky Taylor, co-author of the book, *Be More Kid* (Meyerowitz, 2020).

As we get older, we believe that grownups have all of the answers; but what if the reverse is true? What if, in order to live a meaningful and satisfying life, we need to unlearn the harmful behaviors we've picked up as adults and embrace our inner child?

"We've all had the resources within us all along, not only to help us through difficult times, but to thrive," Nicky says. "We just need to unlearn detrimental adult tendencies and 'be more childlike'" (Meyerowitz, 2020).

So, here are five methods to embrace your inner kid, based upon Nicky Taylor, Mark Taylor, and Ed James' principles (Meyerowitz, 2020):

Re-establish Connection with Lost Dreams

Children think they can be anything they want - they have no doubts that restrict them, and adults around them encourage them to believe everything is possible. As we get older, our goals and prospects vanish and are replaced with "have to's" and "must do's." Those same individuals who previously encouraged our aspirations, now tell us that we need to find something practical to do that pays well or our dreams won't come true.

Get in touch with your childhood dreams. What were they? What was significant to you about the things you used to fantasize about? How could you do something similar as an adult? Why not take classes if you once aspired to be a ballerina? Write those dreams down for yourself and place them somewhere you can be reminded of them.

Rekindle your unflinching faith in yourself and your abilities. Surround yourself with those who believe in you, completely.

The Art and Science of Thinking

Children think in a very simple manner. It never occurs to them that something may go wrong. Obstacles are just non-existent. If you explain why they can't accomplish something, they will tell you all of the ways they can!

Adults, on the other hand, believe their own reasons for not trying something, and if they do push through fears, they frequently wind up feeling guilty or visualizing everything that could go wrong, which ruins their enjoyment of a pursuit. Retrain your mind to concentrate on everything that is going well. To accomplish this, think of something particular that is coming up, and spend some time picturing what the scenario looks like after it has ended. What are you going to see, hear, feel, and think to yourself?

Remember that pleasant image every time you think about that incident—this is the only version you need to envision. Take note of how cheerful and calm you now feel about that occasion, perhaps even a bit eager, like a child might. Once you know how, it's simple to embrace your inner child!

Be Constant

Consider how persistent a youngster is when he or she wants something. They will keep repeating their request until they obtain what they want, no matter how obnoxious it is!

As adults, we may only ask for something once, and if our request is ignored or we do not receive the desired result, we may feel unable to ask again. You don't have to go to such lengths as a child, but if something is essential to you, use that childlike desire to make it happen. Look for an alternative way, put yourself in the shoes of the other person, and discover a win-win situation that benefits both of you. It's your life, you owe it to yourself to live it to the fullest.

Play a lot

Kids are extremely imaginative and can transform almost any situation into a game. They like having fun and easily invite their new best buddy over for a sleepover, despite the fact that they have just recently met them.

Adults, on the other hand, will perform the chores they dislike, miserably, rather than finding a way to enjoy them—even putting off doing the ones that they do enjoy as a result. Find innovative methods to make things you don't like into a game or a competition; you'll be surprised at how fast you can do them when they're enjoyable.

As we age, making new acquaintances can become a significant challenge, and those who are overly pleasant are even considered suspect! Everywhere you go, take advantage of the opportunity to meet new individuals. Simply be yourself and take in the friendliness for what it is. You'd be astonished at how many intriguing stories folks have to share (It would be advisable to wait a little longer before inviting them over for a sleepover!).

Contentment Overhead of Happiness

Kids discover satisfaction in the present moment, getting immersed in what they are doing or will do next. They don't consider anything else. Adults search for happiness outside of themselves or believe they will be happy in the future when circumstances change, such as when they have more money or can retire. As a result, they lose out entirely on the opportunity to be present in the moment.

Maintain complete focus on what you're doing right now. Enjoy the sensation of being in the now rather than waiting to go somewhere else. Instead, simply enjoy the ride that is life.

Key Takeaways

- Creativity is the key to letting the inner child express themself. There are different techniques to be creative from coloring to building with legos. Make sure to try a variety of creative ideas to help your inner kid.
- Your inner child is still a part of you, so they have a right to live a fulfilling life. Working on the above mentioned techniques will help you achieve the goal.
- Recovery from trauma happens in stages, if you feel like it is coming back again, don't lose hope. Keep the practice going.

7

Extra Healing Practices

"Healing is an art.
It takes time.
It takes practice.
It takes love."

— MAZA DOHTA

This chapter talks about:

- A letter to my inner child
- Your inner child's message to you
- The mindfulness energy
- A healing meditation for your inner child

Your inner kid is no longer estranged or lost. However, they still require some healing in order to let go of the past and accept the future. He/she is now grateful to you since you recognized them after all these years, just when they believed they were alone. This chapter outlines additional healing procedures that will be helpful in the healing process.

A Letter to My Inner Child

Your inner child is that part of you, the 'original' self, that still views and responds to the world through the eyes of a child who is innocent (and occasionally hurt).

It's about bringing the fragments of your history into the light of day so you can see what has yet to be resolved—where you have yet to be seen and heard. It's facing your limits and making a peace offering to the pieces of yourself that you've never forgiven. The versions of you who are still bound by past fear, treading water and unable to go on. It's a method to bring softness to your stress, to breathe into your heart's neglected chambers. It's about re-orienting yourself in light of your totality by piecing together your fractured self like a puzzle.

It boils down to becoming a mom to the pieces of yourself that were left behind when the rest of you developed. It's you, lavishing yourself with the love, attention, and approval you never had. It's not an easy job, sorting through the belongings you've been dragging about for far too long. Your recovery is complicated because you are human, and all humans are complicated.

Inner child work may be quite therapeutic if you allow yourself to be receptive to it. You could have a breakdown and then have a breakthrough. You may suddenly realize that the sensitive region behind your right shoulder blade is where the trauma settled when your father died.

Even what you've educated your mind to forget, your body remembers. Fear is stored in the muscles, humiliation in the cells, and sadness in the bones.

Your heart, too, recalls everything. You only need to be quiet enough to hear the facts you've been hiding from yourself, and it's enlightening when you do.

Whatever you've gone through, this letter may be exactly what your younger self requires.

You are the one speaking to your innermost self when you read this. You're speaking to the part of yourself that has been damaged, starved, abused, abandoned, ashamed, left out, and left behind: your inner child.

You're paying attention. You're hearing them. You are present in every facet and season of oneself. Allow yourself plenty of time. Read this letter as though it were your own, because it is yours:

Hello there,

Firstly, I ask for your apology for ignoring you for all these years. In my defense, I was scared of approaching you after the incident and locked you away. With time, I grew to be the best version of me but little did I know that my every decision had an impact on you. Please forgive me for approaching this late, but, better late than never, right?

You felt isolated and misunderstood for many years. You felt that no matter how hard you tried, you were never good enough. Everything seemed to be your fault. I'm writing to affirm your sentiments and let you know you're not alone.

Today is the day we confront your suffering, or, more accurately, our pain, and cut off the old roots.

You did an excellent job of concealing yourself. I now see that this caused you to bottle up all of your feelings and become the person you are today. But don't be afraid to express yourself since today is the day we make a difference.

You are not insane, overly emotional, or too sensitive. Those that told you that, were simply emotionally immature themselves and did not completely comprehend your situation. Please accept that it is not your fault. Your emotions are valid, and you have the right to express them. You needed to defend yourself, and you were doing your best with what you had. I appreciate you for that. You don't have to conceal yourself any longer. You don't have anything to prove.

I know how many times you've suppressed your needs for fear of being condemned for expressing them. I know how many times you've kept your rage disguised when you felt you weren't being treated fairly. And I know how much sorrow that has caused you. You don't have to hang on to this humiliation, disappointment, and anguish any longer. You are not required to hold yourself together anymore.

It's about time to let it go...

I am here for all the re-assurance. I will keep sending the positivity your way so you can heal. You are worthy of being told "I love you." And I am here to make sure that you keep hearing it.

I hope you find the strength inside yourself to remember that your value is not determined by the thoughts and judgments of others, and that you do not need to satisfy anybody in order to be appreciated and adored. I hope you learn to always love and respect yourself even though you were never taught how. I hope you'll now consider yourself a priority in this cruel world.

It's all right to let go.

You're no longer in danger. I'm here to help you, with new information and better tools.

You're still here, and I'm grateful for that. When you point out the locations that still ache, I learn more about what you require. You educate me to pay attention with every sensation of guilt, anxiety, or envy.

I apologize for the things you wish you could have handled better or learned sooner. Please forgive me. Thank you very much. I adore you.

You may forget it from time to time, but you are always loved.

You have always been sufficient.

I haven't always noticed you, but now I do.

I haven't always listened to you, but I am listening now.

Thank you for your courage. When you had so much to cope with, you continued smiling and being friendly. Even when you were in pain, you made people feel seen and heard.

I hope your heart remains open even when you are not treated with kindness. I love you.

Your Inner Child's Message to You

Our minds have the ability to entirely alter our perception of a situation. It contains receptors that are associated with certain types of feelings and are only activated when we experience emotions. Similarly, as children, we retained a feeling of surprise, awe, and innocence in our brains. It never lets us grow old and keeps the spark of excitement alive within us. It keeps us interested in new things, seeking joy, and inspiring astonishment in the world around us. This positivity, however, is out of reach to our inner child who has experienced trauma as a youngster. Instead, feelings of dread, worry, loneliness, or uncertainty dominate their outlook, which then may appear in our thoughts, behaviors, and decisions as adults. When our inner child takes hold in stressful situations and drives us in the incorrect direction based on those sensations, it may wreak havoc on our life.

Those who were traumatized and harmed as children are not the only ones who may have felt unsafe as a youngster. In reality, most people can certainly reflect back on pleasant childhoods and identify areas where their needs were not addressed. There is no such thing as the 'ideal' parent. It's the most difficult duty anybody has, and most parents do their best with the information, education, and maturity they possess. Recognizing where our parents fell short in making us feel secure, isn't a process of assigning blame, rather it's a way for us to become aware of the sensations their lack of protection has caused. A kid may feel unsafe in a variety of ways, including: physical or emotional abuse or neglect, a lack of positive reinforcement, a lack of space for emotional expression, feeling criticism or humiliation, being forced to succeed at a high level, or growing up too fast, to name a few.

Your inner child grows up with you. They grow angrier and more furious with you because you continue to ignore it. Working directly with this part of you (and any other parts within it) may help you to: heal trauma, stop dysfunctional habits, connect with your essence and personal truth, meet your needs, experience joy, and live according to your internal compass, among other benefits. There are several approaches to working with the inner child. One such approach is, allowing your inner child to also send you a letter as though he or she has journeyed across time.

This type of practice can aid in the connection between you and your inner child. As youngsters, there was no open discussion with our parents, and we were often misunderstood. Before we can acknowledge our inner child, we must first understand one of the reasons they "act out" through us—they feel unheard. Examine your upbringing carefully to identify times when your inner child felt unheard or insecure. Connect with them to reassure them that they are protected and provide them a safe space to vent their unpleasant emotions.

Begin drafting the letter to your inner child. Remember, it's almost like talking to yourself, so take it easy. Don't worry about the sentence structure or using difficult words. Be simple. Make sure you are sitting in a comfortable place away from any distractions. Begin brainstorming the feelings you recognize on a sheet of paper. This is only the starting point. From here on out, all of your questions/statements will be based on the core reasons you've identified. Begin by acting as though your inner child is a stranger to you, and you want to learn more about him or her and become friends with them. "Hello, how are you?" is a good place to start. "It's been a long time, and I hope everything is going well with you." These inquiries will sway your inner child's affection towards you and minimize their anger.

Ask your inner child if he or she prefers talking or writing. If they want to write, begin by writing about the event you want to address or the reason you feel led down a different road. If they prefer to converse, stand in front of the mirror and look yourself in the eyes to address the inner child. Don't be afraid or think you're crazy, this is the most effective technique to get your subconscious to listen to you.

Don't be harsh on your inner child and don't place any demands on him/her. Instead, let them speak for themselves and develop a shared foundation of understanding, because all meaningful dialogue is born from mutual understanding. Allow your inner child to voice his or her concerns openly, but you may ask specific questions such as, "Where did it start?" "How has life changed for you?" "How come you didn't reach out to me?" Questions like these can help you better grasp the issue and may lead to a greater knowledge of your inner child. Never forget that your inner child is also full of love and life. They may be furious at first, he/she will soon see the wonderful side of it.

Our inner child needs love and reassurance, just like any other human being. Using reassuring words like, "I will protect you," "I am here for you," and "I have got your back" will calm him/her. It will soothe the negative feelings and create the feelings of safety they previously lacked. This can be further accomplished through guided meditations or visualizations, which are amazing in aiding us to envision ourselves sitting next to our inner child, giving us the ability to imagine hugging and consoling them. You can also indulge your inner child by playing the way they want to, go to a park or amusement park, watch a movie you loved as a child, color, or do any other activity they'd enjoy.

Here is a sample of the letter you can look to for guidance:

Hello there Adult,

It's great to hear from you after such a long time. After all this time, I had given up on the possibility of reconnecting with you and having a heart-to-heart. Growing up brought you many difficulties, which drove you away from me. You're probably in need of a rest and someone to chat to. It amazes me how you seek affection from other people when I am right here. I know you're worried that I've been injured and transformed as a result of that traumatic experience. But you have to believe me when I say that it was just the wrong moment, not the wrong life. I, too, need to appreciate the beauty of life rather than reliving the pain over and over again. I'M OVER IT! You locked me up after the event and continued on with your life, while I was hidden away here, imprisoned. SET ME FREE. Make a difference in your life. Reunite with me to realize your true potential and conquer the world. I'm hoping to get some attention from you before I shut myself away for good.

Practice this exercise of reaching out to your inner child to sort things out. Once you have done it, you will feel content with life. Always remember, you and your inner child will become friends now, so you can reach out for him/her in case of any obstacles. You are now teammates.

The Mindfulness Energy

To repair your inner child, you must first cultivate and nourish your attention so that you can awaken yourself to the truth of your pain, which you would otherwise want to escape. If you choose to pay attention, there are clear warning signs of greater suffering: you've become engrossed in your pain, recounting and retelling your story to anyone who will listen, as though you are competing—my misery is greater than yours. Without realizing it, you are keeping your sorrow alive by courting it.

Continually courting our suffering is an unpleasant romance, as we could find ourselves in a codependent relationship that must be acknowledged by its actual name: addiction. We get physiologically and emotionally entangled in our pain to the point where we cannot live without it, even if it is ruining our well-being. Yes, we clutch for momentary insights—this is suffering—but only when they arise to the surface of our awareness. The buried sorrow, on the other hand, has a way of gaining speed and energy until it suddenly erupts in its entirety— the tiny serpent has grown into a monster. Our mental condition is now infected with an addiction to misery. We react to every sight of sorrow with such destructive emotion that we reinforce the reasons and situations that caused the misery to begin with. As a result, we keep shooting ourselves in the foot—again and again.

Mindfulness is thought to have started some 2500 years ago in ancient eastern and Buddhist philosophy. Jon Kabat-Zinn popularized the notion of mindfulness in the Western world. Kabat-Zinn initially found awareness while practicing Zen Buddhist meditation with Zen Buddhist meditation masters, Philip Kapleau, and Korean Zen Master, Seung Sahn Haengwon. Kabat-Zinn secularized historical Buddhist mindfulness principles by detaching them from Buddhist cultural, religious, and ideological factors and orienting them to the "Western mind" and culture, resulting in the development of the first formalized Mindfulness-Based Intervention (MBI), known as Mindfulness-Based Stress Reduction (MBSR) (Kabat-Zinn, 2003).

The store of consciousness, also known as root consciousness, is the foundation of human awareness. In Western psychology, this is referred to as "the unconscious mind." It is the repository for all of our prior experiences. Store awareness is capable of learning and processing information.

Our minds are frequently absent from our bodies. Sometimes we go through our everyday routines without even thinking about it. We can do a lot with only store consciousness, and mind consciousness can think of a thousand more things. For example, while we drive across the city, our mental consciousness may not be thinking about driving at all, yet we can still arrive at our destination without getting lost or in an accident. That is our store consciousness at work. Awareness is analogous to a home, with the basement representing our store consciousness and the living room representing our mind consciousness. Mental formations such as rage, grief, or joy exist in the store of awareness as seeds. We have seeds of wrath, despair, prejudice, and fear, mindfulness, compassion, understanding, and so on. Store awareness is composed of all of the seeds, and is also the soil that sustains them. The seeds remain until we hear, see, read, or think of anything that reaches a seed, causing us to feel anger, joy, or sadness. In our living room, a seed is sprouting and blossoming on the level of mental consciousness. We no longer refer to it as a seed, but rather as a mental creation.

When someone touches the seed of anger by saying or doing anything that irritates us, that seed of anger rises to the surface and manifests in mind consciousness as the mental formation of rage. My hand is a biological structure. My rage is a mental construct. Seed varieties can appear as mental forms. One of them is anger. Anger is referred to as a seed in store awareness. It's referred to as a mental formation in mind consciousness.

The first thing we may do when a seed, like the seed of anger, rises up in our living room and emerges as a mental formation, is to touch the seed of mindfulness and ask it to come up as well. In the living room, we now have two mental forms. This is angry mindfulness. Mindfulness is always focused on something. Mindfulness of breathing occurs when we breathe thoughtfully. When we walk attentively, we are practicing walking awareness. When we eat consciously, we are practicing mindfulness of eating. So, in this scenario, mindfulness is rage mindfulness. Mindfulness acknowledges and accepts rage.

This technique is founded on the nonduality insight that anger is not an adversary. Both awareness and anger are aspects of us. Mindfulness exists not to repress or combat anger, but to notice and manage it— much like a big brother assisting a younger sibling. As a result, the energy of awareness recognizes and gently embraces the energy of rage.

When we need the energy of mindfulness, we just tap that seed with our thoughtful breathing or mindful walking, give a smile, and then we'll have the energy to undertake the job of identifying, welcoming, and, in time, profoundly transforming. Whatever we are doing, whether it is cooking, sweeping, washing, strolling, or being aware of our breathing, we may continue to produce mindfulness energy, and the seed of mindfulness in us will grow strong. The seed of focus is contained within the seed of awareness. We may free ourselves from ailments by using these two powers.

The Mind Requires Circulation

Toxins are known to exist in human bodies, and build up in our blood if it does not circulate properly. Toxins must be expelled from our bodies in order for us to be healthy. When the blood flows properly, the kidneys and liver can fulfill their jobs of eliminating pollutants. Massage, for example, can be used to improve blood circulation.

Our awareness, too, may be in poor circulation. We may be carrying a poison in our awareness in the form of anguish, agony, sadness, or despair. This is referred to as an interior knot or structure. The technique of massaging our consciousness involves embracing our grief and sadness with the energy of mindfulness. When our blood does not flow properly, our organs are unable to work effectively, and we become ill. When our psyche does not flow properly, our mind becomes unwell. Mindfulness boosts and speeds up circulation throughout pain blockages.

Taking Over the Living Room

Because our blockages of pain, sadness, rage, and despair have grown large and want our attention, they always try to come up into our mental consciousness, into our living room. They want to come out, but we don't want these unwanted visitors since they're terrible to look at. As a result, we attempt to obstruct their path. We'd like them to sleep in the basement. We don't want to confront them, so we fill the living room with other people. We do all we can to keep our living room occupied whenever we have ten or fifteen minutes to spare. We dial a friend's number. We take out a book. We switch on the television. We go for a drive. We are hoping that if the living room is occupied, these nasty thought formations will not arise.

However, all mental forms must circulate. If we don't allow them to surface, they cause poor circulation in our brain, and symptoms of mental illness and sadness begin to show in our mind and body. Doctors often prescribe medicine for physical symptoms, yet might occasionally ignore our internal structures, exacerbating our illness.

Taking Down Obstacles

If we can learn to face our knots of anguish, we may gradually allow them to grow up into our living room. We start to learn how to embrace and change them with the energy of awareness. When we remove the barrier between the basement and the living room, blocks of anguish will emerge, and we will have to be prepared to endure a period of suffering. Our inner child may have a lot of dread and wrath pent up from spending so much time in the basement. There is unfortunately no way around it.

That is why mindfulness practice is so vital. It is really uncomfortable to have these seeds sprout if attention is not paid. But if we know how to produce the energy of awareness, it's incredibly therapeutic to encourage and accept it every day. Mindfulness is a powerful energy source that can detect, welcome, and care for these negative energies. Maybe these seeds don't want to sprout at first because there's too much fear and distrust, so we'll have to encourage them a little. After some time of being embraced, a powerful feeling will return to the basement, inevitably forming a seed again, but this time it will be weaker than before.

Every moment you bathe your internal forms in mindfulness, the barriers of suffering within you dissolve. So, every day, give your wrath, despair, and dread a thoughtful wash. After a few days or weeks of bringing them up regularly and then assisting them to go back down, you build proper circulation in your psyche.

The Purpose of Mindfulness

Mindfulness' primary purpose is to take pause at any time and become aware of the child within us. All we have to do when we first see the wounded youngster is to be aware of him or her and say hello. That's it. Perhaps this child is depressed. If we observe this, we might simply take a deep breath in and tell ourselves, "I realize that grief has manifested in me. Hello, my pity. I will take good care of you," and exhale.

The second role of mindfulness is to accept our inner child after we have identified him or her. This is a really enjoyable practice. Rather than fighting our feelings, we are taking care of ourselves. Concentration is an ally that mindfulness brings with her. The initial few minutes of tenderly identifying and nurturing our inner child will provide some solace. The painful feelings will remain, but we will not suffer as greatly.

The third role of mindfulness, after acknowledging and welcoming our inner child, is to calm and ease our painful emotions. By gently cradling this infant, we may soothe our tough feelings and begin to feel at peace. We will be able to see the origins of these mental constructions when we welcome our powerful emotions with mindfulness and attention. We'll be able to pinpoint the source of our pain. Our suffering will be alleviated if we can recognize the source of the problem. As a result, mindfulness acknowledges, embraces, and relieves.

The energy of mindfulness includes both the energy of concentration and the energy of insight. Concentration allows us to focus on only one subject at a time. The energy of staring gets more powerful with focus, and enlightenment is attainable. Insight has the ability to liberate us at all times. If we can maintain our attention, enlightenment will surely follow. Therefore, the energy of mindfulness allows us to examine ourselves deeply and obtain the understanding we require for transformation.

A Healing Meditation for Your Inner Child

The following meditation will assist in healing from early childhood trauma. Utilize this meditation on a daily basis because it creates a gentle place for the body, heart, and mind to recall. As you will continue to develop and grow in self-love, it will provide a living place of inclusion and compassion for childhood memories and all past experiences.

Make Use of Your Love and Support Resources

Thich Nhat Hanh once reminded us that we can build a good fire with pieces of straw or paper. The straw bits that assist us in developing loving-kindness energy are our resources for, "cooking up love" (Rowe Ward & Ward, 2021).

People, places, pets, activities, and lovely memories that soften our hearts and nurture our appreciation, love, and compassion, are all resources that help us grow self-love. Take a few minutes in your practice to thoroughly recollect such a resource. Make it come to life by engaging your senses.

We are thankful to the intelligent and caring therapists, body healers, and shamans who have assisted us on our journey of transformation and healing. A somatic and trauma-informed therapist may be an invaluable support person for individuals on a spiritual journey. For example, a puppy is a great resource to open hearts. Imagine his weight on your lap and the feel of his fur against your hand. Now imagine his bouncy, jaunty step and smiles. You will feel your body relax when you think about the puppy.

Pay Attention to Your Body

Once we have experienced the good sensations of being in touch with our resources, we pay attention to our body. The body is the initial basis of awareness. We love ourselves by being connected to our bodies and acknowledging the marvel that is our bodies.

Find a spot where you can slow down without being distracted, so you can be aware of your body and breathing with some ease. Practice setting your posture thoroughly so that your breath is easy and you can genuinely be present.

Scan your body from head to toe, paying focused attention to your entire body with care. Invite your body to soften and relax, nestling onto your cushion or chair. According to Thich Nhat Hanh, this is how we maintain our appointments with life. He further suggests, "we halt, we relax, we rest, we heal, and we evolve" (Hanh, 2022). Sending this loving, attentive energy to your body is an act of self-love.

Show Your Inner Child Love

Then, silently, offer yourself these guided meditation words:

- I'm breathing in, and I'm aware that I'm doing so.
- I know I'm breathing out, so I pay close attention to the out-breath.
- As I take a deep breath, I am aware of my entire body, in the present moment.
- As I exhale, I am aware of my entire body, in the present moment.
- When I take a deep breath, I imagine myself as a five-year-old child, frail and defenseless.
- As I exhale, I smile to myself as if I were a five-year-old child.

As a follow-up, you can start a conversation with your inner child, if you would like to proceed a bit further. This meditation has assisted us in seeing ourselves as children and seeing the very genuine fragility of being human. We typically undervalue our resilience and strength, as well as our fragility and susceptibility. They are not distinct. In actuality, our fragility contains tremendous power and strength. While it may not be easy at first, being in touch with vulnerability offers a great opportunity to connect with life and our own goodness. The hidden divine child inside can be healed and strengthened as a result.

Key Takeaways

- Healing takes time so don't get frustrated if the things don't work out in the initial days of your practice. Keep the exercises going and you will soon see the change.
- Your inner child will heal and reach out to you through these techniques.
- Listening to your inner child's feelings and allowing yourself to

experience them rather than pushing them away might help you understand and validate the anguish you've felt.

- Mindfulness can help you heal your inner child as your practice will focus all your energy into its rightful place.

Conclusion

Our inner child is a part of ourselves, which lives within us. They have been there since we were conceived, through utero and all of the developmental years that followed. The inner child frequently remembers both positive and negative childhood events, such as anxieties, traumas, neglect, or profound loss. When we begin to investigate our inner environment, we might begin to see internal patterns that have left us with subconscious "bread crumb trails." Our inner child is always interacting with us...

All we have to do now is learn to listen.

Now, our inner child may either be quiet and comfortable, or they can act out and make things a little rumbly on the inside—impeding good relationships, organizational abilities, and self-regulation.

When it comes to becoming a productive member of society, or taking steps toward pleasure, our inner child may make or break us.

If you're feeling irritated or trapped in your life, it's likely that your inner child requires some care. Stuck spots might manifest as difficulty at work, in parenting, in finding or maintaining love, in growing relationships, or in creating boundaries.

We were all children once, and those children are still alive and well today. Many of them have gone into hiding—waiting for someone to notice their anguish.

They'll be ready to appreciate every moment, carefree and light, once it happens. They want to be able to express themselves. They need to feel protected and loved in order to do so. When they are unable to, it is frequently due to unresolved childhood trauma. These are the bitter memories from your past that you have learned to ignore. In regular life, you might not see them. But it doesn't mean they aren't present.

Unfortunately, your inner child may try to ruin your adult experience by attempting to cope with their unresolved difficulties. However, you can help them to heal by reparenting yourself. This entails offering your inner child the loving presence and self-compassion you wished you had as a child.

What does it mean to reparent your inner child? Reparenting is an effective strategy for mending emotional scars from childhood. In essence, you take on the role of the parent you lacked as a child, emancipating your inner child from the past by providing for yourself what you did not receive as a child.

This is crucial for the development of self-esteem and the healing of emotional wounds from the past. As a result, you will be able to maintain positive connections and live a happy life. You may begin satisfying your developmental requirements yourself after you've become aware of the ways you weren't getting them fulfilled in childhood. Being your own excellent parent is what this entails.

Journaling, writing a letter to your inner child, and drawing, are just a few ways to feel connected with your inner child. Once you build the bridge and feel a connection, you can reparent your inner child as per your wants and needs.

How to Rediscover Your Inner Child?

Most of us have scars from our childhood that need to be healed. Connecting with our inner child may aid in this process, regardless of the amount of trauma our inner child has experienced. Childhood scars can manifest in a variety of ways in our adult lives.

The following are the six ways to rediscover your inner child:

1. identify the neglect
2. accept the past
3. accommodate your inner child
4. reach out to your inner child
5. embrace your emotions
6. fill the gap by taking action

Inner child work has several advantages. It might be especially beneficial for people who experienced general dysfunction, neglect, physical abuse, or sexual abuse as youngsters. Inner child work can assist people in processing trauma by recognizing and resolving the underlying causes of any ongoing psychological scars that interfere with their capacity to function as adults. The following are some of the advantages of inner-child work:

- increased living quality
- relief from depression
- enhanced reactions that are situationally appropriate
- better performance integration of ego states
- improved interpersonal interactions
- increased vitality
- a regained sense of childlike awe
- enhanced emotional control and maturity
- higher levels of genuineness
- a holistic sense of self

We saw the world through a completely different lens as children. As a result, many of the things we believe never wounded us as children, may still have left lasting impressions. This is why it's critical to avoid making assumptions about your inner child.

Through inner child therapy, you may learn to grieve, heal, and resolve whichever causes of trauma you've been knowingly or unknowingly hanging on to for years through your inner child. The practices mentioned within this book, such as: writing a letter to your inner child, a healing meditation for your inner child, five ways to live your best life, having mindful energy, and clearing your root chakra blockages, are some examples of the techniques that will help your inner child to heal!

BONUS: Your Free Gifts

I'm only offering this bonus for FREE to my readers. This is a way of saying thanks for your purchase. In this gift, you will find a guide with extra tools to start your inner journey.

Healing your Inner Child First Guide

Embark on a Transformative Inner Journey to Rediscover Your Inner Child with Extraordinary Tools!

Inside this book, you'll discover:

1. How to use Journaling in the Healing Process.
2. Questions to Remember Your Inner Child.
3. Space to Write Your Thoughts Down.
4. Questions to Better Understand Your Inner Child's Pain.
5. Motivational Things to Say to Your Inner Child.
6. Positive Affirmations + a 5-Step Method to Make Your Own.
7. An Extra Inner Child Meditation.
8. A Checklist.
9. And More...

To receive this extra **bonus,** go to: https://booksforbetterlife.com/inner-child-first

Or scan the QR code:

Thank You

I really appreciate you for purchasing my book!

You had the chance to pick a lot of other books, but you chose this one.

So, **thank you so much** for purchasing this book and reading it to the very last page! I hope that I was able to help you in your healing process, as my goal is to help as many people as possible!

Before you close the book, I want to ask for **a small favor**. Would you please consider *leaving an honest review* about the book? **This would be really helpful for me**, as I'm an independent author and posting reviews is the best and easiest way to support me.

The feedback you provide will help me so I can continue selling, improving, and writing books. **It will mean the world to me to hear from you.**

Go to this book on Amazon and scroll down (mybook.to/healing-your-inner-child-first), or scan the QR code to leave a review:

Amazon US <— —> *Amazon UK*

Amazon CA <— —> *Amazon AU*

References

Anderson, K. (n.d.). *The stages of trauma and recovery.* Clarity Therapy NYC. https://www.claritytherapynyc.com/stages-of-trauma-and-reco very/.

Chen, G. (2020, December 30). *How the arts benefit your children academically and behaviorally.* Public School Review.

Cotec, I. (2020). *Shadow work and healing the inner child (In 5 steps).* HeroRise. https://www.herorise.us/shadow-work-and-the-inner-chil d/.

Diamond, D. (2008, June 7). *Essential secrets of psychotherapy: The inner child.* Psychology. https://www.psychologytoday.com/ca/blog/evil-de eds/200806/essential-secrets-psychotherapy-the-inner-child.

Delagran, L. (n.d.). *How to deal with fear and anxiety.* University of Minnesota. https://www.takingcharge.csh.umn.edu/how-deal-fear-an d-anxiety.

Estrada, J. (2019, October 30). *Reparenting therapy can help you heal your inner child—here's how.* Well+Good. https://www.wellandgood.com/re parenting-therapy/.

Firestone, L. (2022). *Freeing Yourself from childhood trauma.* PsychAlive.

https://www.psychalive.org/freeing-yourself-from-childhood-trauma
/.

Fredrickson, B. (2014). *The science of happiness, theory and practice.* Pursuit of Happiness. https://www.pursuit-of-happiness.org/history-of-happiness/barb-fredrickson.

Hanh, T. (2022). *Body Scan.* Spirituality & Practice Resources for Spiritual Journeys. https://www.spiritualityandpractice.com/pract ices/practices/view/28468/body-scan.

Howie, V. (2021, January 7). *Heal your sacral chakra inner child.* Chakra Boosters. https://www.chakraboosters.com/heal-sacral-chakra-inner-child.

Kabat-Zinn, J. (2003). Mindfulness-based interventions in context: Past, present, and future. *Clinical Psychology: Science and Practice, 10*(2), 144–156. https://doi.org/10.1093/clipsy.bpg016.

Kellend, M. (2015). "Carl Jung." In *Personality Theory in a Cultural Context.* Portland State University. https://pdx.pressbooks.pub/thebal anceofpersonality/chapter/chapter-5-carl-jung.

Meyerowitz, A. (2020, November 20). *Why we should embrace our inner child and 5 ways to do it.* Red. https://www.redonline.co.uk/health-self/self/a34725323/how-to-embrace-inner-child/.

Pandey, S. (2021, December 31). *Break the cycle of trauma: Re-parent your inner child.* The Bliss Key. https://www.theblisskey.com/post/bre ak-the-cycle-of-trauma-re-parent-your-inner-child.

Proyer, R. T., Gander, F., Bertenshaw, E. J., & Brauer, K. (2018). The positive relationships of playfulness with indicators of health, activity, and physical fitness. *Frontiers in Psychology, 9.* https://doi.org/10.3389 /fpsyg.2018.01440.

Robinson, L., Smith, M., & Segal, J. (2018, November). *Emotional and psychological trauma.* HelpGuide. https://www.helpguide.org/articles/ ptsd-trauma/coping-with-emotional-and-psychological-trauma.htm.

Robinson, (2021, July). *Laughter is the best medicine.* HelpGuide. https://www.helpguide.org/articles/mental-health/laughter-is-the -best-medicine.htm.

Rowe Ward, P., & Ward, L. (2021, December 20). *Loving-kindness: healing your inner child.* Lion's Roar. https://www.lionsroar.com/l oving-kindness-healing-your-inner-child/.

Siegel, D. (n.d.). *Reflections on the mindful brain.* https://communityofm indfulparenting.com/documents/research/Siegel-Mindfulness.pdf.

Sjöblom, M., Öhrling, K., Prellwitz, M., & Kostenius, C. (2016). Health throughout the lifespan: The phenomenon of the inner child reflected in events during childhood experienced by older persons. *International Journal of Qualitative Studies on Health and Well-Being, 11*(1), 1062-1071. https://doi.org/10.3402/qhw.v11.31486.

Snowise, K. (2015). *Authenticity: Are you embracing your true-self?* Thrive.How. https://thrive.how/authenticity-are-you-embracing-you r-true-self/.

Stelter, G. (2016, December 18). *A beginner's guide to the 7 chakras and their meanings*. Healthline. https://www.healthline.com/health/fitness-exercise/ 7-chakras.

Thoughtless Delineation. (2018, December 27). *Moving on from childhood trauma*. Medium. https://medium.com/thoughtless-delineation/moving-on-from-childhood-trauma-e222b9c7e28b.